Contents

Foreword

History books are often filled with names and dates—words and numbers for students to memorize for a test and forget once they move on to another class. However, what history books should be filled with are great stories, because the history of our world is filled with great stories. Love, death, violence, heroism, and betrayal are not just themes found in novels and movie scripts. They are often the driving forces behind major historical events.

When told in a compelling way, fact is often far more interesting—and sometimes far more unbelievable—than fiction. World history is filled with more drama than the best television shows, and all of it really happened. As readers discover the incredible truth behind the triumphs and tragedies that have impacted the world since ancient times, they also come to understand that everything is connected. Historical events do not exist in a vacuum. The stories that shaped world history continue to shape the present and will undoubtedly shape the future.

The titles in this series aim to provide readers with a comprehensive understanding of pivotal events in world history. They are written with a focus on providing readers with multiple perspectives to help them develop an appreciation for the complexity of the study of history. There is no set lens through which history must be viewed, and these titles encourage readers to analyze different viewpoints to understand why a historical figure acted the way they did or why a contemporary scholar wrote what they did about a historical event. In this way, readers are able to sharpen their critical-thinking skills and apply those skills in their history classes. Readers are aided in this pursuit by formally documented quotations and annotated bibliographies, which encourage further research and debate.

Many of these quotations come from carefully selected primary sources, including diaries, public records, and contemporary research and writings. These valuable primary sources help readers hear the voices of those who directly experienced historical events, as well as the voices of biographers and historians who provide a unique perspective on familiar topics. Their voices all help history come alive in a vibrant way.

As students read the titles in this series, they are provided with clear context in the form of maps, timelines, and informative text. These elements give them the basic facts they need to fully appreciate the high drama that is history.

The study of history is difficult at times—not because of all the information that needs to be memorized but because of the challenging questions it asks us. How could something as horrible as the Holocaust happen? Why would religious leaders use torture during the Inquisition? Why does ISIS have so many followers? The information presented in each title gives readers the tools they need to confront these questions and participate in the debates they inspire.

As we pore over the stories of events and eras that changed the world, we come to understand a simple truth: No one can escape being a part of history. We are not bystanders; we are active participants in the stories that are being created now and will be written about in history books decades and even centuries from now. The titles in this series help readers gain a deeper appreciation for history and a stronger understanding of the connection between the stories of the past and the stories they are part of right now.

SETTING THE SCENE: A TIMELINE

1006 ···· 1492 ···· 1620 ···· 1685 ···· 1881 ···· 1914–1918 ···· 1939–1945 ····

The Islamic conquest of Xinjiang sparks a refugee crisis.

Anti-Jewish pogroms take place in Russia.

World War II creates millions of refugees.

King Louis XIV of France revokes the Edict of Nantes, sending Huguenots into exile.

The Pilgrims, religious exiles from England, land in America.

Word War I takes place, causing millions of deaths across the globe.

Spanish monarchs Ferdinand and Isabella issue their Edict of Expulsion, forcing Jews to leave Spain.

1948 .... **1950** .... **2003** .... **2015** **2017**

The Office of the
United Nations High
Commissioner for
Refugees (UNHCR)
is established.

President Donald
Trump fights to
limit or ban
refugees from
primarily Muslim
countries from
entering the
United States.

The United States invades
Iraq; war rages in Darfur
between religious groups.

The Palestinian
exodus takes place.

Thousands of persecuted Muslims
flee Myanmar and Bangladesh,
creating the Rohingya refugee crisis.

THE REFUGEE IN HISTORY

The controversy over accepting refugees into the United States was crystalized in one conversation between American president Donald J. Trump and Australian prime minister Malcolm Turnbull in January 2017. Trump had campaigned on a platform that would be highly restrictive of refugees from certain parts of the world because he believed that would make America safer. At one point in his presidential campaign, he shared his thoughts on taking in refugees from Syria: "We have to stop the tremendous flow of Syrian refugees into the United States … We don't know who they are. They have no documentation and we don't know what they're planning."[1]

After assuming the presidency, however, Trump was in a bind. In the final months of the Obama administration, the United States had agreed to accept up to 2,000 refugees that were being held in Australian camps. The refugees had come from countries such as Iraq, Iran, Somalia, and Sudan, which were countries from which Trump had recently attempted to ban immigration to the United States. Trump was angry that Turnbull still wanted to hold him to the promise made under Obama. In a conversation that became heated, Trump told Turnbull that accepting the refugees "will make me look terrible."[2]

There Have Always Been Refugees

Such disagreements have always been at the heart of the refugee question. There is almost always a tension between parties who want to resettle refugees and those who do not want to allow them into "their" country. The refugee crisis in the 21st century is a worldwide problem. Conflicts in Syria, Afghanistan, Iraq, Myanmar, Sudan, the Democratic Republic of the

Congo, and elsewhere have touched off mass migrations and altered the landscape of world population and politics. The backlash against the acceptance of refugees is not limited to the United States. Great Britain's exit from the European Union, commonly referred to as Brexit, was largely a reaction to the country's acceptance of Middle Eastern and African immigrants and refugees. In Germany, the rise of the far-right group Alternative for Germany (AfD) has likewise been a response to Chancellor Angela Merkel's policy of accepting foreign refugees.

While the refugee crisis has exploded in the 20th and 21st centuries, with the number of worldwide refugees now more than 20 million (when including people displaced within their own countries, the number is more than 65 million), refugees have been seeking shelter from the storm since the dawn of mankind. One chronicler of the history of religious refugees, Frederick A. Norwood, suggested that humans have been refugees since Adam and Eve were expelled from the Garden of Eden in the Bible's book of Genesis. "Man, metaphorically speaking, has been a refugee ever since,"[3] he observed.

Norwood goes on to suggest that the next generation of human history outlined in the Bible "also resulted in a 'refugee movement.'"[4] After murdering his brother Abel, Cain is sent into exile. Norwood noted that "even in exile, [Cain] was under the providential care of God, who placed his seal upon him to protect him."[5] This seal has symbolic importance for today's refugees: International law mandates that refugees must be protected. How effective such protections are—in an era when the numbers of those in need far exceed nations' abilities to offer them safe harbor—is an open question.

Who Is a Refugee?

At a time in history when more refugees need more aid than ever, even the very word "refugee" has come under scrutiny. Both the definition of the word "refugee" and, consequently, who qualifies for help, are matters of debate. For most of human history, there was no central organization dedicated to providing assistance to the world's refugees. Prior to the mid-20th century, the exiled peoples of the world were essentially on their own. Many would argue that they still are. However, in 1950, responding to those displaced in the aftermath of World War II and others fleeing Communist persecution in Europe, the Office of the United Nations High Commissioner for Refugees (UNHCR) was established. The UNHCR was initially charged with protecting and assisting such peoples, but toward the end of the century, its focus shifted to aiding refugees from Africa, Asia, and Latin America. In

UNHCR workers register many refugees on the Greek island of Kos off the coast of Turkey.

recent years, the Middle East has been added to that list. In 1951, the United Nations Convention Relating to the Status of Refugees formulated a definition of "refugee" that is still used today. This definition reads:

A refugee is someone who has been forced to flee his or her country because of persecution, war, or violence. A refugee has a well-founded fear of persecution for reasons of race, religion, nationality, political opinion or membership in a particular social group. Most likely, they cannot return home or are afraid to do so. War and ethnic, tribal and religious violence are leading causes of refugees fleeing their countries.[6]

There are a few key parts of this definition. It states that in order to gain refugee status, people must have fled across the physical borders of their homeland. Victims of internal displacement, or exile within their own country, are not included. Additionally, the definition makes no provision for those who are fleeing the ravages of civil war and other conflicts but are not directly threatened. Because, by international law, those classified as refugees receive "certain rights not available to other international migrants, including the right of resettlement and legal protection from deportation or forcible return to his country of origin (the so-called *non-refoulement* protection),"[7] the precise definition of a refugee is highly important to those seeking asylum.

The 1951 treaty has been signed by 145 nations and still provides

Displaced Syrians, such as these children, often head to refugee camps.

SMUGGLED INTO EUROPE

The following is a real account of one refugee's difficult journey from his home country:

In the darkness far out to sea, Hashem al-Souki can't see his neighbours but he can hear them scream. It's partly his fault. They are two African women—perhaps from Somalia, but now is not the time to ask—and Hashem is spreadeagled on top of them. His limbs dig into theirs. They want him to move, fast, and so would he. But he can't—several people are sprawled on top of him, and there's possibly another layer above them. Dozens are crammed into this wooden dinghy ... It is perhaps eleven at night, but Hashem can't be certain. He's losing track of time, and of place. Earlier in the evening, on a beach at the northernmost tip of Egypt, he and his companions were herded into this little boat. Now that boat is who-knows-where, bobbing along in the pitch darkness, lurching in the waves, somewhere in the south-eastern Mediterranean. And its passengers are screaming.

Some of the screams are in Arabic, some not. There are people from across Africa here, others from across the Middle East. There are Palestinians, Sudanese and Somalis. And Syrians, like Hashem ... They want to get to northern Europe: Sweden, Germany, or anywhere that offers them a better future than their collapsed homelands. For that distant hope they are risking this boat trip to the Italian coast. All being well, they should reach Italy in five or six days. But, for now, Hashem doesn't know if he'll survive the night. Or if anyone will.

An hour passes. They reach a second boat, a bigger one, and then a third, bigger still. At each new vessel, the smugglers toss them over the side like bags of potatoes. Now they have a bit more space, but they're soaked. They had to wade through the waves to get to the dinghy, and the second boat was full of water. Their clothes drenched, they shiver. And they retch. The person squeezed to his left pukes all over Hashem. Then Hashem pays the favour forward, spewing all over the person to his right. He looks up, and realises everyone's at it; everyone's clothes are caked in other people's vomit. Each has paid more than $2000 to spew over fellow refugees. "It's a vomiting party," Hashem thinks to himself.[1]

1. Patrick Kingsley, *The New Odyssey: The Story of Europe's Refugee Crisis*. New York, NY: Norton, 2017. PDF e-book.

the international laws according to which refugees are treated. As professors Alexander Betts and Paul Collier wrote, "It was unambiguously a product of its time and place, explicitly temporary and at the time intended only to apply to people in Europe." But, as Betts and Collier continued, "Time did not stand still."[8] Thus, many argue that the UNHCR's definition of a refugee is inadequate in the 21st century. As Gil and Ann Dull Loescher wrote, "The stark fact that must be faced is that the world is witnessing a huge growth in forcibly displaced people ... In terms of sheer numbers, non-Convention 'refugees' fleeing civil wars, ethnic conflicts, and generalized violence ... are a bigger problem for the international community than [those who fit the UN definition]."[9]

Several subsequent statements on refugees have widened the definition to become more inclusive and take into account a greater refugee population. The Convention on Refugee Problems in Africa in 1969 defined victims of "external aggression, internal civil strife, or events seriously disturbing public order"[10] in Africa as refugees. The Cartagena Declaration of 1984 included "persons who have fled their country because their lives, safety, or freedom have been threatened by generalized violence, foreign aggression, internal conflicts, massive violation of human rights, or other circumstances which have seriously disturbed public order."[11]

Aiding Contemporary Refugees

The UNHCR is still the main international group that deals with refugees, but it is not alone. The International Committee of the Red Cross assists people caught in conflicts, the World Food Program coordinates food aid to refugees, and the United Nations Children's Fund (UNICEF) aids women and children. There are also a host of non-governmental agencies (NGOs) worldwide that conduct studies on the global refugee situation and provide aid. "As implementing partners for the UNHCR, NGOs bear the brunt of delivering food and providing shelter, water, sanitation, and health care to refugees."[12]

Despite the heroic efforts of such organizations, the sheer numbers of refugees in the early 21st century has far exceeded the ability of these organizations to help them. As Betts and Collier have argued, "even according to its own metrics, the refugee system is failing badly."[13]

The relatively few refugees who do make it to safer environments would not know that, however. Once they arrive in the United States, for example, refugees receive services from a wide range of charitable organizations. In just one small city in upstate New York, for example, there are numerous refugee aid organizations.

Many refugees are grateful for the chance to build a new life in the United States.

These include Catholic Family Center, the Jewish Federation, Mary's Place, Refugees Helping Refugees, Saint's Place, No One Left Behind, Muslim Volunteer Network, and Refugee Resettlement Services. There is also a school, the International Academy, that serves hundreds of refugee students. Many of the organizations that aid refugees have expanded their services over time. For example, Mary's Place has grown from a coat distribution center to a full service refugee aid organization.

Refugees who make use of such services are often extremely grateful. When asked what they like about coming to America, many cite simple pleasures such as a bed, having soap, towels, and shampoo—things most Americans take for granted. They also cite greater pleasures: food on the table, good schools, and peace.

CHAPTER ONE

EARLY REFUGEES

Even though the term "refugee" was not legally defined for international use until the 1950s, there have always been refugees. As Gil Loescher wrote, "[Refugees] have been a political as well as a humanitarian issue for as long as mankind has lived in organized groups where intolerance and oppression have existed."[14] Loescher, Alexander Betts, and James Milner have observed that "wars, political upheavals, ethnic discrimination, religious strife and a wide range of other human rights abuses lead people to become refugees."[15] Human history is full of stories of forced migration and exodus, and the importance of respecting and protecting asylum seekers is a part of many religious traditions and holy texts. In ancient cultures, sites of worship were noted for granting asylum to those fleeing wars, political upheaval, and religious persecution. Many

secular (non-religious) texts and traditions also affirm the importance of assisting those who are on the run from oppression.

Refugees in Classical Times

As evidenced by the literature of ancient Greece, the issue of asylum was very much a topic of frequent discussion. Numerous works of literature, from Homer's *Odyssey* to Sophocles's *Oedipus at Colonus*, focused on the idea of a desperate outcast seeking shelter from strangers. The Greeks cherished the idea of hospitality, or *xenia*, which is the idea that it was one's duty to treat foreigners with courtesy and generosity. When Oedipus, blind and banished from his homeland of Thebes, shows up in Colonus (near Athens), Theseus, the king, offers unconditional aid. In Homer's *Odyssey*, when a naked and desperate Odysseus washes up on the shore of Scheria, home of the

Phaeacians, he is shown the utmost courtesy, even though doing so angers the god Poseidon, who has a grudge against the hero. While such tales are more myth than history, they provide a blueprint for how the Greeks ideally expected foreigners to be treated.

This was probably not the case in actual practice, however. As historian Robert Garland wrote, "Of the many thousands who became homeless in the Greek world, a few could seek shelter, either temporarily or permanently, through ... *xenia*, though to what extent [this]

In Homer's Odyssey, *Odysseus, desperate and alone, is shown hospitality by his Phaeacian hosts.*

institution did much to alleviate the hardship of the average refugee or migrant is questionable."[16] For ancient Greeks, even those living in the relative peace of a city such as Athens, the chance of being forced from their homes represented a very real danger. In fact, during many large-scale wars, that danger became a harsh reality for many Greeks.

Wandering was a constant in ancient Greece. "From earliest times," Garland wrote, "the Greeks were in restless movement, propelled from their familiar habitat either by human force or by ... their environment. And so it remained throughout antiquity."[17] There were no statistics on refugees in the ancient world, but displacement was a regular event, and the majority of refugees "disappeared without a trace once they had severed ties with their homeland."[18] This is partly because no historian of the time was much interested in charting the wanderings of commoners. As Garland argued, "Even if some enterprising Greek had invented the newspaper, I seriously doubt that refugees would have made the headlines. No one ... ever concerned himself with ... the 'global implications' of war, famine, and disease for the thousands of victims of such disasters."[19] It is known, however, that a lot of famous Greeks were forced to move and seek asylum in lands other than their homeland. These included the philosopher Aristotle, the mathematician Pythagoras, the playwright Euripides, and the historian Thucydides.

In the later Roman times, as well, refugees were highly common, and the Romans could be somewhat sympathetic to the plight of the displaced. This is not surprising, given the Roman Empire's origins. As author Richard Miles observed, "A major element of their own mythical backstory centred on the wanderings of their legendary founder, the Trojan prince Aeneas, who with a small group of companions and close family had been the only survivors of the Greeks' apocalyptic destruction of his home city"[20] in the Trojan War.

The prosperous and extensive Roman Empire was regularly flooded with refugees numbering in the tens or hundreds of thousands. The Romans, who continually needed new sources of labor, were often glad to accept foreigners into their fold. Refugees who were not a political or military threat could be treated reasonably well. They helped work farms, served as soldiers, and worked as artisans across the empire. One Roman ruler—Emperor Caracalla—even granted full Roman citizenship to anyone born free in the empire, no matter their parents' birthplaces.

Changing Times

This generous policy toward refugees changed over the course of Rome's

ARCHAEOLOGISTS DISCOVER A ROMAN ERA REFUGEE CAMP

In 2011, archaeologists working in the area of Hadrian's Wall—a barrier built by the Roman Empire to keep out foreign invaders—discovered what they believed to be a refugee camp dating from the third century AD. Andrew Birley, who directed the archaeological dig, said, "These are very unusual buildings and it looks as though they may number into the hundreds. Events clearly took place here on a large scale to lead to this sort of construction."[1] Archaeologists speculate that the refugee camp would have been inhabited by tribespeople fleeing south from a societal breakdown north of the Roman border. If so, the refugees might have served the dual purpose of feeding the Roman troops as well as providing a human barrier between Scottish enemies to the north and Roman fortifications along Hadrian's Wall. In return, the Romans may have offered protection from hostile parties in the north. "Maintaining a buffer zone occupied by friendly tribes after the invasion was part of imperial strategy and would have justified heavy spending on refugee care"[2] as the Roman army invaded Scotland. Birley added, "It would make sense to bring refugees behind the curtain of Hadrian's Wall to protect them for so long as fighting continued. They would have had real value to the Romans who always protected anyone and anything valuable to them."[3]

This picture shows the remains of Hadrian's Wall in Northumberland, England.

1. Quoted in Martin Wainwright, "Hadrian's Wall dig unearths Roman refugee camp," *Guardian*, June 20, 2011. www.theguardian.com/science/2011/jun/20/hadrians-wall-roman-britain-refugee-camp.
2. Wainwright, "Hadrian's Wall."
3. Quoted in Wainwright, "Hadrian's Wall."

history, and many historians believe that a refugee crisis along the eastern border of the empire may have helped bring about Rome's collapse. It has surprised historians that the Romans dealt with a refugee crisis so poorly, seeing as they had handled so many similar situations in the past, using refugees to help the empire thrive and expand. As author Eric Scigliano observed, "The Romans were hardly novices at resettling refugees and other immigrants. Theirs was the world's longest-running multi-ethnic, multinational society, the most diverse and successful ever seen—at least until the rise of [the United States]."[21]

In the fourth century, a massive group of Goths (from eastern Germany) was pushed to the eastern border of the Roman Empire by an army of marauding Huns, warriors feared throughout the region as fierce fighters with no mercy. The Goths settled in on the far bank of the Danube River, in what is now Turkey. "For the Romans," Richard Miles wrote, "this looked like a win-win situation: free manpower to address the chronic shortage in the imperial Roman army. What followed, however, was a total catastrophe."[22] Overwhelmed by the sheer number of Goths, who totaled as many as 100,000, the Romans tried to keep them on the far side of the Danube. The Goths remained there for months, living in terrible conditions. They began raiding the surrounding countryside for food. Stories were told of Goth parents trading their children to the Romans in exchange for dog meat in an effort to avoid starvation.

This ugly situation led to the Battle of Adrianople in Turkey, near the border of Bulgaria and Greece. The eastern Roman army, led by Emperor Valens, fought against the Goths. The battle resulted in an overwhelming victory for the Goths and the death of Valens. Many historians view the Battle of Adrianople as a signature moment directly leading to the fall of the Roman Empire. They point out that, had the Romans treated the Goths with some dignity, the sequence of events that doomed the empire might not have been set in motion.

There is also one important instance in which the Romans caused a refugee evacuation instead of dealing with foreign refugees. Roman persecution of Christians is well documented, and the martyrdom of scores of Christian zealots is central to the religion as it is known today. Historian Frederick A. Norwood explained that historians' focus on individual Christian martyrs who stayed and were executed has obscured the number of refugees who escaped Roman persecution: "How many fled to the mountains for a while? ... How many migrated to begin life anew in a land of a foreign tongue? Who knows?"[23]

Wandering Jews

Like the early Greeks and Christians, the Jewish people have a history of wandering. The image of the wandering Jew has its first iconic moment in the Biblical story of Cain. The ancient Exodus from Egypt, when a band of Jewish refugees escaped and wandered in the desert for 40 years before arriving at the "promised land," is a familiar story. Still another refugee crisis occurred in the 8th century BC. After the Assyrians invaded ancient Israel, the Jews were on the move again.

Another key moment in the Jewish diaspora (or scattering of people) came in AD 70, when the Romans sacked Jerusalem, destroying the city's temple and leaving only part of the famous Western Wall. According to Norwood, "The [Jewish] movement out of Palestine was of a twofold nature. First was the immediate forced emigration. Second was a slower voluntary emigration as conditions became hopeless. Palestine ceased to be a focus for Jewish living."[24]

Perhaps the most well-known Jewish refugee crisis occurred around the time of the Spanish Inquisition. Spanish rulers Isabella and Ferdinand may have gone down in history for their role in promoting Christopher Columbus's explorations of modern-day North America, but their ruthlessness in dealing with the Jews is also well documented. Victims of continuous persecution in Catholic Spain, the Jews had been leaving by the thousands before 1492, when Ferdinand and Isabella issued their Edict of Expulsion, also known as the Alhambra Decree.

Jews were given the option to convert to Catholicism, and as many as 200,000 became conversos (Spanish for converted) in order to remain in the country. Despite converting, however, many Jews were still not safe. The Spanish Inquisition sought to root out those who had made a show of converting but were not truly followers of the Catholic faith. Those Jews who would not convert fled to Portugal, Navarre, the French region of Provence, Italy, and North Africa. Not long after, these countries also made declarations expelling the Jews. Ultimately, many of the Jews from Spain (also called Sephardim) sought refuge in the Ottoman Empire, where they found the Muslim people to be much more welcoming and hospitable. Many found a new home in cities such as Istanbul, Smyrna, and Edirne, far away from Spain, as Jewish communities and temples sprang up in the East. The general consensus is that Ferdinand and Isabella's edict ultimately caused more than 100,000 Jews to leave the country.

Though the Jews thrived among the Ottomans, getting to these distant lands could be a terrible experience. Such was the case for Don David ibn Yahya, who was born in Lisbon,

This Francisco de Goya painting depicts a scene from the Spanish Inquisition.

Portugal, in about 1440. A wealthy entrepreneur and distinguished scholar who authored several books, Yahya was accused of asking conversos to return to the Judaic faith. As a result, he was forced to flee Portugal and, in doing so, give up most of his wealth. At first, he found refuge in Naples, Italy, but after Naples was conquered by Spain in 1495, he was forced to flee again. He set out for the Ottoman Empire, where his uncle had fled before him, but he lacked the funds to complete the trip. In Corfu, Greece, he was forced to sell his belongings, including a rare book collection, to continue the journey. He did eventually reach the relative safety of Istanbul (now in Turkey), but he lived the rest of his life in poverty.

Conditions were scarcely better for the conversos who remained in Spain. The Spanish Inquisition was building momentum, designed to root out heretics and those who were not Christian enough to satisfy church officials. Prejudicial Spaniards came up

EXPELLED FROM SPAIN

The following is an excerpt from the infamous Edict of Expulsion, which created a massive refugee crisis as Jews were forced from their Spanish homeland:

> We order all Jews and Jewesses of whatever age they may be, who live, reside, and exist in our said kingdoms and lordships, as much those who are natives as those who are not, who by whatever manner or whatever cause have come to live and reside therein, that by the end of the month of July next of the present year, they depart from all of these our said realms and lordships, along with their sons and daughters, menservants and maidservants, Jewish familiars, those who are great [nobles] as well as the lesser folk [commoners], of whatever age they may be, and they shall not dare to return to those places, nor to reside in them, nor to live in any part of them, neither temporarily on the way to somewhere else nor in any other manner, under pain that if they do not perform and comply with this command and should be found in our said kingdom and lordships and should in any manner live in them, they incur the penalty of death and the confiscation of all their possessions.[1]

1. "The Edict of Expulsion of the Jews," Edward Peters, trans., Foundation for the Advancement of Sephardic Studies and Culture, accessed December 26, 2017. www.sephardicstudies.org/decree.html.

with a new term for Jews who they believed had publicly converted to Christianity but were still practicing Jewish traditions in private: Marranos (Spanish for pig). Many of these Marranos ultimately escaped Spain and Portugal in the 16th and 17th centuries out of fear.

The Jews were allowed back into Spain in the 19th century, but the infamous Edict of Expulsion was not formally revoked by the Spanish government until 1968. It is worth noting that in 2015, Spain passed a law offering dual citizenship to descendants of Sephardic Jews expelled from the country in 1492.

The Huguenots Flee France

The Huguenots were French Protestants who followed the teachings of John Calvin. France, like Spain, was ruled by Catholics, and conflicts were inevitable, particularly since Huguenot teachings held that the monarchs were not supreme rulers. In their belief system, Biblical laws trumped all. As the Huguenots' numbers grew

and they continued
to defy the French
crown, a series of re-
ligious wars erupted.
These became known
as the French Wars
of Religion from the
1560s to the 1590s.
The wars ended with
the Edict of Nantes in
1598, which granted
France's roughly
2 million Huguenots
the freedom to wor-
ship openly, among
other concessions.
Tensions with the
Catholic Church and
the monarchy nev-
ertheless continued,
and in 1685, King
Louis XIV declared
Protestantism illegal
with his Edict of Fon-
tainebleau, popularly
known as the Revo-
cation of the Edict
of Nantes.

This proclamation,
devastating to the
French Protestant
population, had an
enormous effect. Ref-
ugees poured into
England, Ireland,
Holland, Belgium,
Germany, Scandi-
navia, Switzerland,

French Huguenot refugees after the Revocation of the Edict of Nantes are depicted here.

Russia, Austria, Africa, and the Americas. Some historians estimate that 200,000 Huguenots fled France, but others put the number as high as 800,000. Those who fled included teachers, philosophers, farmers, merchants, lawyers, bankers, industrial leaders, and soldiers. This not only weakened the intellectual and economic core of France, it also strengthened these fields in other European countries with more lenient religious policies.

Realizing the extent of the exodus, Louis XIV tried to close France's borders. Ships were intercepted and officials were ordered to report suspicious movements by Protestants. This did not stop the flow of refugees, but it did make it much more difficult to find peace. Families were often separated on the journey, as they were forced to stow away on ships or disguise themselves to get past French authorities.

As with the Jewish refugees from Spain, the Huguenots often made major contributions to their new communities, though they often arrived penniless. Their skills allowed them to thrive in places such as Protestant England. Historian Massimo Livi-Bacci, who estimates that only 140,000 to 160,000 Huguenots fled France, observed that while the demographic consequences of such migration were slight (France's population numbering as much as 20 million in those times), the

economic and social impact was immense. Instead of helping France move forward, "the Huguenots contributed to the development of tapestry, glass, paper, and agriculture in Brandenburg; silk, gold, and clock-making in England; and banking in Switzerland."[25]

Famous descendants of Huguenot refugees include American actor Johnny Depp, British prime minister Winston Churchill, American folk hero Davy Crockett, Irish Nobel Prize–winning author Samuel Beckett, Swiss philosopher Jean-Jacques Rousseau, American general George S. Patton, and South African actress Charlize Theron.

The *Muhacirs* Flee to Turkey

At its height, the Ottoman Empire was one of the most powerful on Earth. With its capital in Constantinople (now Istanbul) and its policy of relative religious tolerance, it was a safe haven for foreign refugees, whether they were Christian, Jewish, or Muslim. At its peak, the Ottoman Empire included vast stretches of southeast and central Europe, western Asia, northern Africa, the Caucasus, and the Horn of Africa (which includes modern-day Ethiopia and Somalia). A series of unending wars and rebellions took a toll on the Ottoman Empire, and by the 19th century, it was in serious decline and it had lost the

Actor Johnny Depp traces his ancestry back to the French Huguenots.

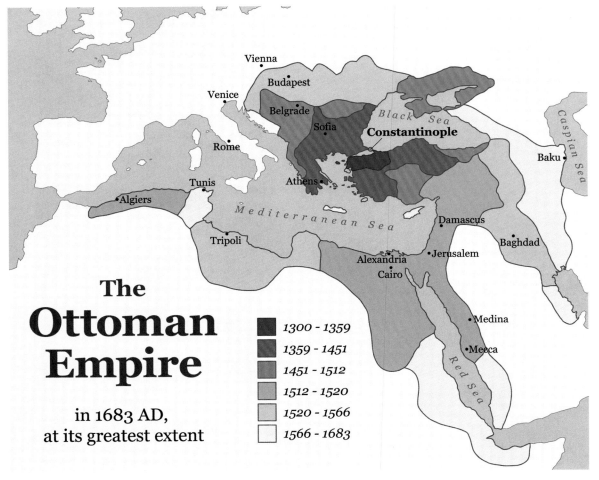

The Ottoman Empire

in 1683 AD,
at its greatest extent

	1300 - 1359
	1359 - 1451
	1451 - 1512
	1512 - 1520
	1520 - 1566
	1566 - 1683

This map shows the extent of the Ottoman Empire in the 17th century.

respect of other European and Asian countries. As the Ottomans lost conflicts, a massive migration of at least 5 million Muslims was set in motion that continued for well over a century. These people were called *muhacirs*.

There was one significant problem with this mass migration. As Feroz Ahmad observed,

The Ottomans were a rare imperial people who had no homeland to retreat to as their empire waned in the nineteenth and twentieth centuries. Other imperial peoples had returned to various homelands: the British to their island base ... the French to France, the Spanish to Spain, and so on. By the twentieth century, the Ottomans had no homeland for they had originated as tribal peoples who, for a variety of reasons, had been forced to migrate from the steppes of Central and Inner Asia and went in different directions.[26]

As their empire grew weaker, Muslim refugees from Caucasus, Crimea, Crete, Greece, Romania, and Yugoslavia flooded into what is now Turkey. As Suraiya Faroqhi wrote,

In many cases, Ottoman territorial losses were coupled with expulsions and emigration. Some Muslims emigrated in a reasonably orderly fashion, but many more had to flee due to acts of war and massacres of the Muslim population, which were part and parcel of the wars of independence in the Balkans. Entire populations ... were forced to emigrate after the annexation of their territory by the Russians in 1863. The refugees often lost everything they owned.[27]

Modern-day Turkey became the refugees' home. Today, the *muhacirs'* descendants make up between one-fourth and one-third of Turkey's population of 80 million people.

Other Major Refugee Migrations

These examples of mass migrations—due to religious conflict, economic woes, and intolerance—are but a few of the countless such refugee crises that occurred prior to the 20th century.

In 1006, the Islamic conquest of the Buddhist kingdom of Xinjiang led to a mass migration of refugees. These refugees traveled west along the famed Silk Road, a vital trade route between China and what is now Iran and India. These refugees brought new technology and religion to the West.

The Romany peoples, otherwise known as Gypsies, began migrating from India in the 13th century. They had been treated as outsiders and placed in the lowest social class in India due to their unique culture. Of course, they continued to be outsiders in Europe as well. Nazi Germany attempted to permanently exterminate their culture, forcing them into ghettos and, later, concentration camps. As many as 500,000 Romany people died during this time.

The Pilgrims who landed at Plymouth in 1620 were religious refugees who braved the dangerous journey to North America in order to escape persecution and worship freely in the new world.

Pogroms in Russia caused a mass exodus of Jews from the 1880s into the early 1900s. Many Jews escaped to America. By 1920, as many as 400,000 Jews had settled in the crowded tenements of New York City's Lower East Side in Manhattan. Despite the scale and scope

Jewish refugees are shown here in New York City around 1900.

of pre–20th century migrations of refugees, all of these movements were but precursors to those of the last century. With the advent of two world wars and political upheaval rampant in the modern world, refugee crises would explode worldwide.

Chapter Two

EARLY 20TH–CENTURY REFUGEE MOVEMENTS

The 20th century saw an ever-increasing number of refugees—from the Armenian victims of Turkish oppression and genocide to the Russians fleeing the Russian (or Bolshevik) Revolution of 1917, as well as the European masses displaced by World War I. Early 20th–century refugee crises differed from those of earlier eras in two distinct ways: First, in the sheer numbers of refugees, with as many as 1 million Armenians, 1.5 million Russians, and 1.8 million Europeans fleeing their respective crises; second, with the emergence of nation-states, refugees were no longer able to cross easily into other lands and merge with an existing population. Refugees in the 1900s increasingly found borders closed, and countries that formerly offered asylum were now unwilling to accept them.

For example, in the 1700s and early 1800s, the United States encouraged open immigration. By the late 1800s, however, the country began to pass laws barring certain immigrants. The Chinese Exclusion Act of 1882 and the Alien Contract Labor Law of 1885, for example, prevented large migrations of foreigners. Anti-immigrant backlash in the early 20th century led to the institution of a quota system in 1921 and then the Immigration Act of 1924, which severely limited the immigrant flow to the United States. Prominent politicians of the era leveraged a fear of immigrant workers "stealing" work from Americans into their campaigns. This culture of fear contributed to a national attitude of mistrust and hatred toward immigrants, despite the country's long history of successful refugees.

Edward Said, a Palestinian American professor who taught at Columbia University until his death in 2003, was among the most elegant

Although refugees have faced closed borders in some places, they have also been met with support from many people around the world.

spokespersons for the refugee in the modern world. In his famous essay "Reflections on Exile," he wrote, "Exile is strangely compelling to think about but terrible to experience. It is the unhealable rift between a human being and a native place, between the self and its true home: its essential sadness can never be surmounted."[28] He goes on to argue, "Modern Western culture is in large part the work of exiles, émigrés [political exiles], refugees. In the United States, academic, intellectual and aesthetic thought is what it is today because of refugees from fascism, communism, and other regimes given to the oppression and expulsion of dissidents."[29]

Before such important contributors to culture, as well as those who simply wanted to live out ordinary

Edward Said, a Palestinian American professor, activist, and scholar, often spoke in support of refugees.

lives in obscurity, could ever settle into a new existence, they had to endure some of the most horrific trials that cruel and powerful governments could devise.

Mass Displacement During World War I

World War I launched a humanitarian crisis unlike anything ever witnessed before. The conflict, then called the Great War—because no one at the time considered that there would be another world war—set in motion catastrophic changes in the European population. Though historians put the number of international refugees during World War I at under 2 million, they estimate that the total number of displaced persons (including those displaced in their own countries) was at least 7.5 million. "As Germans and Russians fought for dominance," journalist Chase Gummer wrote, "millions of noncombatants fled, seeking safety … As German soldiers moved east into Russia in 1915 … ethnic-minority groups living near the border fled farther into the interior of Russia … While they were Russian [citizens], refugees from the borderlands often had foreign customs and spoke little or no Russian."[30] One sympathetic observer stated, "Society has renounced the refugees, as if they were a vile disease that can be mentioned only in private and in hushed tones."[31]

Over the course of four years, each new offensive by the Allies or the Central Powers—the two warring forces—set in motion new floods of refugees throughout Europe. The Russian army's incursion into Austrian Galicia, now part of Ukraine, in 1914 forced many refugees to flee toward Vienna, Austria. As the Germans moved in Belgium, a similar exodus occurred. Hundreds of thousands of Belgians and French fled south into unoccupied France. Even the end of World War I in 1918 did not alleviate the torrent of refugees. If anything, it increased European migration. People who had been driven from their homes during the fighting were now trying to return. However, many villages and cities were completely destroyed—causing these refugees to once again try to find a new home.

The war did have at least one positive result: It led to the rise of numerous relief organizations dedicated to helping former prisoners of war and other refugees. Among these were President Herbert Hoover's American Relief Administration, the International Committee of the Red Cross, and the American Friend's Service Committee. The newly formed League of Nations—the predecessor to the modern United Nations—was formed and helped millions of displaced people. Norwegian explorer Fridtjof Nansen was its first High Commissioner, and he would be

These refugees during World War I are shown carrying all the possessions they could take with them.

instrumental during the Armenian refugee crisis soon to come.

The unprecedented population movements during and after World War I caused problems for the negotiators responsible for remapping the borders of Europe once the war ended. As Gummer wrote, "Most of their successor states contained … thousands of ethnic minorities who had previously belonged to a neighboring country. This added to ethnic strife and fostered the growth of violent … nationalism, ultimately setting the stage for World War II."[32] The World War I refugee crisis would inevitably lead to the even more traumatic refugee crisis of World War II.

Refugees from the Russian Revolution

World War I was particularly difficult for Russian commoners. Warding off the Central Powers and defending their homeland caused the Russians to devote every available resource to the war effort. Russian citizens suffered throughout the war, enduring extreme hardship and even starvation. The setting was ripe for revolution. Czar Nicholas II, who could not successfully manage the domestic crisis set in motion by the war, was overthrown.

In the fall of 1917, Vladimir Lenin and the Bolsheviks (a Communist political party) assumed power in the former Russian Empire, beginning the era of the Soviet Union. Having taken power from the provisional government that had been set up after Nicholas II's fall from power, the Bolsheviks were afraid of losing control themselves. So, under Lenin, Leon Trotsky, and future Soviet leader Joseph Stalin, they were determined to exterminate all potential rivals. In 1918, they murdered former czar Nicholas II and his entire family to ensure that the monarchy would never reappear in Soviet Russia. Ruthlessness was the order of the day for the Bolsheviks. In forming the Red Army in 1918, Leon Trotsky's chilling words summed up

the Bolshevik philosophy: "Root out the counterrevolutionaries without mercy, lock up suspicious characters in concentration camps … Shirkers [slackers] will be shot, regardless of past service."[33]

Those in the west of Russia flooded into European cities. In the east, they moved into China, only to be uprooted again when China eventually became a Communist state. According to historian Erik R. Scott,

Those fleeing Soviet rule had their citizenship revoked, but became the world's first legally recognized refugees, acknowledged by the League of Nations as a group who faced persecution and were deprived of the protection of a state. Being classified as a refugee entitled migrants to certain benefits, including a Nansen passport, a travel document that allowed those without citizenship to cross international borders.[34]

High school teacher Zinaida Zhemchuzhnaia recalled the mass movement of refugees after it became clear that the Bolsheviks would overcome the counterrevolutionary forces—called the Whites—during the Russian Civil War that followed the revolution. First, the soldiers retreated: "Tens of thousands of healthy, well-armed people [were] abandoning the front. The formerly cohesive military units [of the Whites] turned into an undisciplined, disorganized mob, each individual concerned only with his own personal salvation."[35] These soldiers were followed by "carts with refugees, an endless Gypsy camp of women, children, and baggage. Dirty tarps protected the carts from the sun and the rain. Food was cooked in pots over braziers, and clothes were hung around to dry. Trash and excrement were thrown out into the streets."[36] Russia's population suffered greatly as a result of the Russian Civil War. As many as 3 million people fled the

Shown here is a large group of Russian refugees in 1919.

bitter fighting. Zhemchuzhnaia's account suggested that atrocities were common.

Among the Russians who left as first-wave émigrés during this time were pianist and composer Sergei Rachmaninoff, Jewish painter Marc Chagall, novelist Vladimir Nabokov, aviation pioneer and aircraft designer Igor Sikorsky, and more than a million others.

Numerous refugee aid groups stepped in to help those fleeing the Bolsheviks. International organizations, foreign governments, and philanthropists stepped in to help

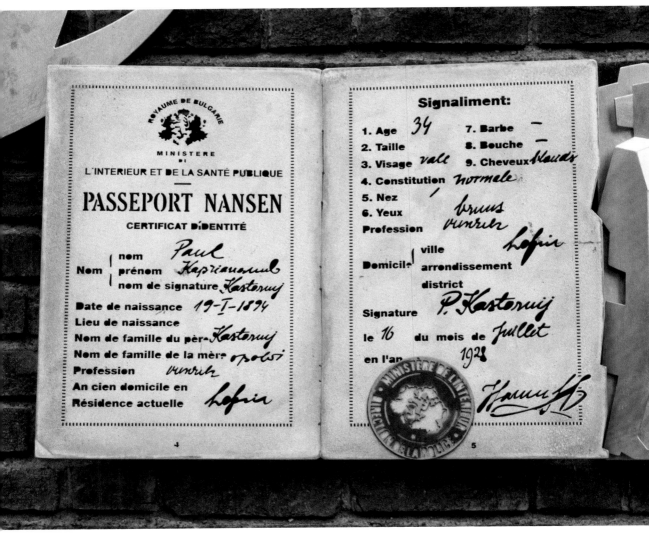

Pictured here is a Nansen passport, initially issued to Russians and then to other refugees.

alleviate the poverty, uncertainty, and isolation of the refugees. The London-based Russian Refugees Relief Association (RRRA) was established in 1920, immediately after White Army forces were evacuated from the Crimea. Czechoslovakia started the Russian Aid-Action program, while the League of Nations issued Nansen passports (named after the high commissioner) to refugees so that they might travel and apply for visas and residence permits. American organizations, such as the YMCA and Red Cross, distributed food, clothing, medical

BOLSHEVIK RUTHLESSNESS AND ORDINARY RUSSIANS

At first, many Russians had high hopes for the Bolshevik regime, which would eventually lead to the creation of the Soviet Union. High school teacher Zinaida Zhemchuzhnaia, herself a future refugee, recounted the moment she and many like her became disillusioned:

> *At five o'clock a rally was convened in front of the town hall. The [Red Army] commissar, who was completely drunk, caught sight of the priest in the crowd. He told him to come closer and then, without saying a word, pulled out his revolver and killed him right on the spot. The crowd gasped. That kindly old priest was beloved by the townspeople … After the brutal murder of the priest there were no more illusions. The Bolsheviks had shown their true face.*[1]

The Bolsheviks' campaign of mass killings, torture, and systematic oppression sent thousands into exile. The civil war that erupted in subsequent years only added to the misery. The Whites, or counterrevolutionary forces, were the largest of several armed groups opposing the Bolsheviks between 1918 and 1921, but they suffered heavy losses and, eventually, defeat. Their sympathizers were anti-Communists who were forced to flee the ruthless Soviet government.

1. Zinaida Zhemchuzhnaia, "The Road to Exile" in *In the Shadow of Revolution: Life Stories of Russian Women from 1917 to the Second World War*, Sheila Fitzpatrick and Yuri Slezkine, eds. Princeton, NJ: Princeton University Press, 2000, p. 103.

aid, and educational materials, and established nurseries and orphanages. Émigré institutions such as the reconstituted Union of Zemstvos and Towns, or Zemgor, previously responsible for running much of Russia's war effort, set up clinics and schools. The Veterans Union, established by Russian general Pyotr Nikolayevich Wrangel, and other associations helped members resolve both legal and practical problems.

Long-term answers to the Russian refugee crisis were hard to come by, however. Within a few decades, the political repression by Adolf Hitler in Europe and the Japanese in China would throw these once safe refugee havens into turmoil once again.

The Armenian Genocide and Its Refugees

The Ottoman Empire had been known for its relative generosity to foreigners in earlier times, and its willingness to accept and incorporate a diverse group of refugees was highly respected. As the empire shrank and ultimately broke up in the early 20th century, all of that changed drastically. The Armenian genocide of the 1900s is one of the bleakest historical moments of its era, and it served as a precursor to the terrors of the Holocaust. Armenians were an ethnic minority in the Ottoman Empire, which absorbed their homeland of Western Armenia in the 1500s.

The beginning of this brutal mass murder is typically dated to 1915, when Ottoman authorities arrested more than 200 Armenian intellectuals and leaders from Constantinople (now Istanbul) and deported them almost 300 miles (483 km) east to Ankara, now the capital of Turkey. Most were subsequently murdered. There were two phases to the genocide, which was carried out while World War I was raging in western Europe: First was the massacre of the able-bodied male population; this was followed by the elimination of women, children, the elderly, and the infirm, who were sent to the Syrian desert.

To this day, the government of Turkey denies accusations of genocide. According to journalist Andrew Finkel, the official Turkish view "is that Turks were themselves the initial victims of ethnic cleansing [genocide]. Armenian revolutionaries, operating behind the [Russian] advance in 1914 … into Ottoman territory, mopped up a Turkish population now caught on the wrong side of enemy lines."[37] The government further argues that "if blame is to be [given] it falls on Armenian revolutionaries who disturbed centuries of coexistence between Muslims and Armenians."[38]

Even following that argument, however, the Turkish response was excessive beyond all reason. Rather than fighting the specific Armenians who took arms against the Ottomans, which is an acceptable, if violent, response by a national government, the empire instead tried to eliminate the entire ethnic population. This resulted in the deaths of hundreds of thousands of innocent noncombatants.

No matter its title—genocide or self-defense—the effects of Turkey's actions are still of consequence today. No one knows exactly how many Armenians were killed, though 1 million to 1.5 million is the estimate commonly given. Similarly, the exact number of refugees is unknown. According to scholar Reşat Kasaba, "Migration emerged as the most common experience of an overwhelming majority of households

ARMENIAN ORPHANS IN CANADA

Shuttled from orphanage to orphanage, many young Armenian refugees died. Others were luckier. A group of 109 were accepted, quite reluctantly, since they were "undesirables," in Canada (like the United States, the Canadians began restricting certain groups of immigrants in the 1920s). The Canadian secretary of the Armenian Relief Fund, A. J. Vining, had written a desperate plea for help:

> *A cry comes from eternity. A million murdered Armenians are pleading with Civilization to care for the battered remnant of an ancient race... A cry comes out of the East. Two hundred and fifty thousand little children are asking for a chance to live. They are the orphans of Armenia. Their fathers and mothers were murdered by the Turks; and now they feebly clutch at life, in weariness and hunger. Across the world they knock timidly at your door for mercy. Will you not answer their appeal?*[1]

1. Quoted in Lorne Shirinian, "Orphans of the Armenian Genocide with Special Reference to the Georgetown Boys and Girls in Canada" in *The Armenian Genocide Legacy*. New York, NY: Palgrave Macmillan, 2016, p. 55.

in Turkey and the other states that succeeded the Ottoman Empire. The experience of moving was etched into the very fibre of all the national communities created in the Balkans and the Middle East."[39]

Historians commonly place the number of Armenian refugees at around 300,000, but some go as high as half a million. Their descendants have largely been scattered across the globe, part of what is now called the Armenian diaspora. Many have remained in the region, but others fled to safety in Europe and America. Thousands were later forced to migrate again; prejudice knows no borders. The Armenian refugees, like many peoples in similar situations, suffered unspeakable cruelty. At best, they were herded into refugee camps in what is now Syria. At worst, they were murdered.

Death and Orphans

With so many adult Armenians now dead, their children were left alone. Many were taken into Muslim households and put to work. Other orphans were left to wander the streets. Organizations such as the Armenian Refugees Fund and Near East Relief stepped in to rescue the stranded children. More than

Armenian refugees often had no choice but to rest at shelters, such as the one pictured here.

100,000 children were rescued and brought to orphanages in Greece, and the task of caring for these children was monumental. Disease was extremely common among Armenian orphans, who rarely had access to hygienic living conditions or a reputable medical facility, as was malnourishment.

Aid for the Armenians sometimes came from unexpected places. Norwegian explorer, human rights advocate, and leader of the League of Nations Fridtjof Nansen, who would win the Nobel Peace Prize for his refugee relief efforts, assisted the Armenian people in 1924. He was tireless in his efforts to get them the aid they needed and to try to find a solution to the refugee crisis. Nansen eventually wrote two books about what he saw. In *Armenia and the Near East*, he observed, "There are descriptions by eyewitnesses of the scenes among these starving and dying people which are so full of heartrending horror that they read like a nightmare."[40] He raised money for the Armenians, and his work led to the eventual relocation of tens of thousands of refugees in Soviet Armenia, Lebanon, Syria, and elsewhere. In recognition of his work, the United Nations created the Fridtjof Nansen Refugee Award in 1954.

CHAPTER THREE

WORLD WAR II AND "DISPLACED PERSONS"

The history of refugee protection goes back to ancient times, but as Gilbert Jaeger, former director of protection for the UNHCR, wrote, "The history of international protection starts with the League of Nations."[41] The League of Nations has generally been regarded as an ineffective organization because its primary mission was to keep the peace, but it could do nothing to prevent the outbreak of World War II. However, the league did prove reasonably effective in aiding refugees. In the aftermath of World War I, millions of refugees, many from Russia but also new asylum seekers displaced by the wars in the Caucasus and the Greco-Turkish War, were in need of aid. Other Europeans, as well as refugees from the Armenian genocide, were still in desperate situations. According to Jaeger, "Emergency relief was provided mainly by charitable organizations. However, these

organizations could not extend their [support] beyond material assistance."[42] Additionally, these charitable groups had limited resources, and perhaps most important, there was no central body that could coordinate relief efforts. In June 1921, Fridtjof Nansen was appointed as the League of Nations High Commissioner for Refugees. In addition to his ongoing work with the Armenians, Nansen directed the League of Nations' first major humanitarian operation: the return to their own countries of some 450,000 European prisoners of war.

After Nansen died in 1930, the Office of the High Commissioner for Refugees was replaced by the Nansen International Office for Refugees. Its aim was to continue the relief work done by its predecessor. In the 1930s, the Nansen International Office for Refugees aided asylum seekers in central and southeastern Europe,

Though refugee camps gave some relief to those fleeing war and persecution, they were often dangerous and overcrowded.

France, Syria, and China. It ran refugee camps, issued Nansen passports to the stateless (which allowed undocumented refugees to travel), and provided visas, jobs, medicine, and food. For its work, the organization was awarded the 1938 Nobel Peace Prize.

Numerous problems beset the Nansen International Office for Refugees during its short existence (1931–1939), however. It lacked adequate financing, the Great Depression of the 1930s cut off refugee employment possibilities, the League of Nations lost prestige once it became apparent that its efforts at keeping the peace were futile, and it could not keep up with the explosion of refugees—mostly from Germany, Italy, and Spain—that accompanied the rise of fascism in Europe. The Nansen Office was replaced by the Office of the High Commissioner of the League of Nations for Refugees and the Intergovernmental Committee on Refugees. These organizations were tasked with many of the same duties as the Nansen Office and suffered many of the same difficulties.

Even the massive refugee migrations of the Great War and its aftermath paled in comparison to what lay ahead. World War II shook the world like nothing that had ever happened before, and in many ways, since. A flood of asylum seekers was unleashed on the world both during and after the conflict, and whereas the refugees from World War I numbered in the hundreds of thousands or millions, newly caused mass migrations could be measured in tens of millions.

The Second World War

Historians estimate that more than 40 million people were displaced in some form or other during World War II. Not all would have been considered refugees by strict definitions, but all of them suffered. The war unleashed devastation on Europe unlike anything seen before. The horrors of World War I looked tolerable compared to the sheer destruction of World War II.

Each time Nazi Germany invaded a country, its occupation set in motion a wave of refugees. Poland, France, Belgium, Luxembourg, and the Netherlands all fell to the Nazi war machine. However, as the German military conquered one nation after another, fleeing became more and more challenging:

Fewer passenger liners crossed the Atlantic Ocean. Those that did left from neutral ports, such as Lisbon, Portugal. In German-occupied Poland, the SS prohibited Jews from emigrating. Jews in Germany could legally leave until fall 1941. It was still possible until fall 1942 for some refugees to leave France to travel to the United States ... Out of fear that the Nazis could smuggle spies and saboteurs in with refugees, immigration officials [in the United States] tightened visa policies for immigrants.[43]

Niels Bohr and Danish Refugees

In 1940, the Germans defeated Denmark's forces in less than a day. One Dane who lived under the Nazi occupation was the famed physicist Niels Bohr, a recipient of the 1922 Nobel Prize in Physics. He was the first to describe the structure of the atom and how to control it to produce nuclear energy. As a man of Jewish descent himself, Bohr despised the Nazi regime. His laboratory in Copenhagen, Denmark, had become a refuge for Jewish scientists who had fled the Nazis. After the German invasion of Denmark, however, no one of Jewish heritage was safe anymore.

Bohr invited another brilliant physicist to visit his lab: the German scientist Werner Heisenberg. In conversation, Heisenberg let Bohr know

This is a monument to Jewish refugees Albert Einstein and Niels Bohr in Moscow, Russia.

that he was working on harnessing the atom for destructive use. He expressed his conviction that the war would be ended by the use of such a device. Bohr was shocked and worried. Both the Germans and the Allied nations respected him and knew that his input into an atomic project could potentially make a big difference in which nations developed the first atomic weapon. Bohr did not believe, however, that building such a weapon was possible. The Germans did. Bohr was not a practicing Jew, but that did not matter to the Germans, so they sought to arrest him as part of a roundup of Danish Jews and bring him to Germany to aid their cause.

When Bohr found out this plan, he fled Denmark. Before he did, he used his leverage as a potential aid to the Allies in their nuclear quest. He petitioned the king of Denmark to let the Danish Jews travel to Sweden, where they would be safe from the Germans, as Sweden maintained a policy of neutrality during the war. As he fled Denmark for the United States, he knew that thousands of Danish Jews would also escape the Nazis.

When Bohr arrived in the United States, he learned that the country's nuclear program was further along than he could have possibly conceived. He agreed to help the Allies develop a nuclear weapon, which was eventually used to conclusively end World War II after the destruction of the Japanese cities of Hiroshima and Nagasaki.

The Rejection of Holocaust Refugees

The United States, like many potential host nations, had long been paranoid about accepting refugees. This statement was no less true in the 1940s. This is not to say that no German Jews made it to the country, however. About 85,000 Jewish refugees entered the United States between March 1938 and September 1939. Unfortunately, many desperate people were also turned away.

In 1939, the German ship *St. Louis* left Hamburg, Germany, with more than 900 passengers, almost all of them Jewish asylum seekers. Bound for Cuba, the boat was captained by a non-Jewish German, Gustav Schröder, a courageous man who

was sympathetic toward the Jews aboard and made sure they were treated well. In Cuba, almost all of the refugees were denied entrance due to visa issues. When the ship subsequently attempted to sail to the United States and then Canada, it was turned away. U.S. Secretary of State Cordell Hull had advised President Franklin Delano Roosevelt not to accept the refugees, and in Canada, immigration official Frederick Blair persuaded Canada's prime minister, William King, to reject the Jews.

The ship was ultimately forced to return to Europe, but Schröder knew that taking them back to Germany would mean a trip to a concentration camp and likely a death sentence. Instead, he brought them to Antwerp, Belgium, and the refugees ended up in England, Belgium, France, and the Netherlands. After Germans occupied the latter three nations, many of the boat's passengers were killed. This small group of refugees was just one of many, as 6 million Jews were eventually murdered by the Nazis, and their story is emblematic of how the world turned its eyes away from preventing the Holocaust.

Once the war began, and even after photographic evidence revealed what the Germans were doing to the Jews, the United States, under Roosevelt, continued to turn away thousands of Jewish refugees, fearing that some might be German spies. For such

Shown here are prionsers in a Nazi concentration camp in Germany.

conspiracy theorists, an incident in 1942 confirmed their suspicions. In the summer of that year, Herbert Karl Friedrich Bahr, a 28-year-old from Germany, arrived in America with a group of Jewish refugees, claiming that he was a victim of Nazi persecution. When authorities questioned him further, they learned that the Germans had paid Bahr to infiltrate the United States and steal American industrial secrets. According to historian Daniel A. Gross, "What Bahr didn't know, or perhaps didn't mind, was that his story would be used as an excuse to deny visas to thousands of Jews fleeing the horrors of the Nazi regime."[44] Bahr was tried as a spy and convicted, and thereafter, the United States used his case as a way to deny entry to countless Jewish refugees, even though there was little to no evidence that any of them were paid German spies. Since

JEWISH DISPLACED PERSONS AFTER WORLD WAR II

Even before the war ended, the Allies had tried to prepare for their eventual victory. They wanted to send the war's displaced persons home as soon as possible, and millions of people were able to return after the war, including many Jews. Still, about 1.5 million people, including about 75,000 Jews, had nowhere to go. For many Jews, everything from their previous lives had been destroyed.

Such people were put in refugee camps, but conditions were often nearly as bad as those faced in Nazi concentration camps. Anti-Semitism (prejudice against Jews) was common, and some of the soldiers who oversaw the camps were not immune to feeling hatred toward the people they were supposed to help.

Allied soldiers regarded German and Austrian Jews as former enemy nationals—in other words, the enemy—and these people were often treated worse than Jews from other countries. Some Jews found themselves in the same refugee camps as former concentration camp guards, who were also considered war refugees.

then, this attitude of paranoia has been applied to other groups of refugees trying to enter the United States. For example, many have claimed that refugees from Muslim nations might be terrorists despite overwhelming evidence to the contrary.

As a result, during World War II, "immigration restrictions actually tightened as the refugee crisis worsened," Gross wrote.

Wartime measures demanded special scrutiny of anyone with relatives in Nazi territories—even relatives in concentration camps. At a press conference, President Roosevelt repeated the unproven claims from his advisers that some Jewish refugees had been coerced to spy for the Nazis. "Not all of them are voluntary spies," Roosevelt said. "It is rather a horrible story, but in some of the other countries that refugees out of Germany have gone to, especially Jewish refugees, they found a number of definitely proven spies."[45]

Many objected to this speculation. Some said it was a case of persecuting refugees for no reason other than the fact that they were from a different country. One magazine, the *Nation*, argued that the State Department could not "cite a single instance of forced espionage."[46] Nevertheless, the paranoid and suspicious voices won out, and desperate European refugees were the victims.

Other European Refugees

Jews were far from the only people fleeing the fighting and turmoil that engulfed Europe during the war and afterward. Charles Simic, a Serbian, grew up in Belgrade, in the former Yugoslavia. He eventually escaped to America, where he was renowned as a poet. As a boy, he said, "Germans and the Allies took turns dropping bombs on my head while I played with my collection of lead soldiers on the floor. I would go boom, boom, and then they would go boom, boom."[47] He also claimed that his imitation of a heavy machine gun was famous in his neighborhood.

When the war ended,

much of Europe was divided up, and Joseph Stalin claimed a large part of Eastern Europe for the Soviet Union. Simic and his family would eventually flee Soviet oppression. "As you sit watching bombs falling in some old documentary, or the armies advancing against each other," he later wrote, "you forget about the people

Charles Simic, a Soviet bloc refugee from the former Yugoslavia, went on to become a famous poet.

huddled in the cellar."[48]

Like so many refugees before and after him and like so many desperate young people who were lucky enough to find comfort in a foreign nation, Simic grew up to make a major contribution to his newly adopted country. A poet, who for many years taught at the University of New Hampshire, he won the Pulitzer Prize in 1990, and in 2007, he was named poet laureate of the United States. He has written of his former status as a refugee with a poet's discerning eye and unique voice. "My family, like so many others, got to see the world for free thanks to Hitler's wars and Stalin's takeover of Eastern Europe,"[49] he wrote. As for his writing, which has a heavy emphasis on history, he explained, "I'm sort of the product of history; Hitler and Stalin were my travel agents. If they weren't around, I probably would have stayed on the same street where I was born. My family, like millions of others, had to pack up and go, so that has always interested me tremendously: human tragedy and human vileness and stupidity."[50]

Finding Asylum Wherever They Could

All told, World War II and its aftermath displaced around 40 million people. The stories of Niels Bohr and Charles Simic are exceptional, but there are millions more who suffered greatly and whose stories will never

be told. In desperate times, people seek shelter wherever they can find it. One largely forgotten story concerns Europeans who escaped the war by journeying to the Middle East. "They journeyed across the Eastern Mediterranean, a trip filled with peril," wrote journalist Ishaan Tharoor. "But the promise of sanctuary on the other side was too great."[51] The refugees included citizens from Bulgaria, Croatia, Greece, Turkey, and the former Yugoslavia. Refugee camps in Egypt, Palestine, and Syria housed tens of thousands of Europeans and were run by the Middle East Relief and Refugee Administration.

Similarly, Iran offered safe harbor for Polish refugees from German terror and Soviet work camps. Hundreds of thousands of Poles journeyed to Iran in the years after Germany invaded Poland. In Iran, these desperate people were often greeted warmly. A Polish schoolteacher, upon arriving in Iran, stated, "The friendly Persian people crowded round the buses shouting what must have been words of welcome and pushed gifts of dates, nuts, roasted peas with raisins and juicy pomegranates through the open windows."[52]

Once the war was over, most of the refugees returned to their homelands in Europe. Unfortunately, the generosity shown toward the European refugees in the Middle East has not always been returned. Tharoor wrote that now, 70 years

REFUGEE CAMPS IN SYRIA

While no one wants to live their life in a refugee camp, these small settlements were often the only opportunity for Europeans who were fleeing from the ravages of war. In the Middle East, where many of these camps welcomed refugees warmly, life in a camp had its ups and downs:

> Once registered, recent arrivals wound their way through a thorough medical inspection. Refugees headed toward what were often makeshift hospital facilities—usually tents, but occasionally empty buildings repurposed for medical care—where they took off their clothes, their shoes and were washed until officials believed they were sufficiently disinfected.
>
> Some refugees—such as Greeks who arrived in the Aleppo camp from the Dodecanese islands in 1944—could expect medical inspections to become part of their daily routine.
>
> After medical officials were satisfied that they were healthy enough to join the rest of the camp, refugees were split up into living quarters for families, unaccompanied children, single men and single women. Once assigned to a particular section of the camp, refugees enjoyed few opportunities to venture outside. Occasionally they were able to go on outings under the supervision of camp officials.
>
> When refugees in the Aleppo camp made the several-mile trek into town, for example, they might visit shops to purchase basic supplies, watch a film at the local cinema—or simply get a distraction from the monotony of camp life. Although the camp at Moses Wells [in Egypt], located on over 100 acres of desert, was not within walking distance of a town, refugees were allowed to spend some time each day bathing in the nearby Red Sea.[1]

1. Evan Taparata and Kuang Keng Kuek Ser, "During WWII, European refugees fled to Syria. Here's what the camps were like," Public Radio International, April 26, 2016. www.pri.org/stories/2016-04-26/what-it-s-inside-refugee-camp-europeans-who-fled-syria-egypt-and-palestine-during.

European refugees during World War II did whatever they could to find a safe place to live.

later, "the positive memory of their Middle Eastern [aid] features little in contemporary conversations now about the current influx of Muslim migrants entering Europe—Poland's right-wing government has been [strongly] opposed to housing any Syrian refugees."[53]

CHAPTER FOUR

THE LATE 20TH CENTURY

The establishment of the Office of the United Nations High Commissioner for Refugees (UNHCR) was a direct result of the post–World War II refugee crisis. Though the UNHCR has often been overwhelmed by the sheer number of refugees, displaced persons, and stateless persons, it has established a series of rules for dealing with refugee situations, and it has provided aid for millions of affected people around the world. The UNHCR continues to do its work into the 21st century, as the world has seen no shortage of refugees.

The Work of the UNHCR

Established in 1950, the UNHCR's original goal was to deal with the European refugee crisis. Its aims have since expanded to include all parts of the world, including Africa, Asia, the Middle East, South America, and more. The UNHCR was not well supported, philosophically or financially, in its early stages. The United States in particular hoped that the agency would outlive its usefulness in a few years and not continue to drain dollars by supplying material aid and funding refugee resettlement indefinitely. Originally, therefore, the organization was charged to work only with those who had become refugees prior to January 1, 1951. Additionally, the UNHCR's authority was supposed to last only until the end of 1953. The reality of an ever-expanding refugee situation—which quickly became global—caused the countries funding the UNHCR to continue their support.

By the end of the 20th century, the UNHCR had not only survived almost 50 years after its initial expiration date but had expanded its mission so that it now dealt with five major categories of people in need: refugees, fleeing their home countries

The headquarters of the UNHCR can be found in Geneva, Switzerland.

in fear for their safety; internally displaced persons, who have been forced to flee their homes but still remain within their native country's borders; stateless persons, who can claim no nationality; returnees, who have fled their homes and then come back; and asylum seekers, who have claimed refugee status but whose cases have not yet been reviewed.

The UNHCR's work has been endless. It has been "one of the lead humanitarian agencies for some of the major emergencies in post-war history—in the Balkans, which produced the largest refugee flows in Europe since the Second World War; in the aftermath of the Gulf War; in Africa's Great Lakes region; and in the massive exoduses in Kosovo and Timor-Leste."[54] In the 21st century, the UNHCR's key function is "international protection—trying to ensure respect for refugees' basic human rights, including their ability to seek asylum, and to ensure that no one is

WHAT IS STATELESSNESS?

The established international definition of a stateless person is "a person who is not considered as a national by any State under the operation of its law."[1] In other words, a stateless person is someone who does not have a nationality. While it is possible to be born stateless, it is more common for an established citizen to become stateless.

According to the United Nations, there are many ways a person can be born or become classified as stateless:

1. *Gaps in nationality laws are a major cause of statelessness. Every country has laws that establish under what circumstances someone acquires nationality or can have it withdrawn. If these laws are not carefully written and correctly applied, some people can be excluded and left stateless. An example is children who are of unknown parentage in a country where nationality is acquired based on descent from a national. Fortunately, most nationality laws recognize them as nationals of the state in which they are found.*

2. *Another factor that can make matters complicated is when people move from the countries where they were born. A child born in a foreign country can risk becoming stateless if that country does not permit nationality based on birth alone and if the country of origin does not allow a parent to pass on nationality through family ties. Additionally, the rules setting out who can and*

returned involuntarily to a country where he or she has a reason to fear persecution."[55] The idea that no one should be forcibly returned to a dangerous country (which would be refoulement, from the French meaning to turn away) is an important principle in modern refugee protection. When Jewish refugees were forced to return to Europe during World War II, the potential for them to be forced into a death camp was a real threat. Refoulement is something that contemporary refugee assistance organizations attempt to avoid at all costs.

The UNHCR acknowledges three desirable options for refugees. They are: voluntary return to their home country in safety, local integration in their new country of asylum, or resettlement in a third country that is neither their homeland nor their current country of asylum. Numerous *who cannot pass on their nationality are sometimes discriminatory. The laws in 27 countries do not let women pass on their nationality, while some countries limit citizenship to people of certain races and ethnicities.*

3. *Another important reason is the emergence of new states and changes in borders. In many cases, specific groups can be left without a nationality as a result and, even where new countries allow nationality for all, ethnic, racial and religious minorities frequently have trouble proving their link to the country. In countries where nationality is acquired only by descent from a national, statelessness will be passed on to the next generation.*

4. *Finally, statelessness can also be caused by loss or deprivation of nationality. In some countries, citizens can lose their nationality simply from having lived outside their country for a long period of time. States can also deprive citizens of their nationality through changes in law that leave whole populations stateless, using discriminatory criteria like ethnicity or race.*[2]

1. UNHCR, "Ending Statelessness," UNHCR, accessed December 26, 2017. www.unhcr.org/en-us/stateless-people.html.
2. UNHCR, "Ending Statelessness."

factors play into where refugees can settle permanently. Every attempt is made not to overwhelm any particular country with a flood of refugees. The UNHCR works with a number of other organizations to facilitate refugee integration into their new society.

The UNHCR and other refugee aid groups were continually challenged by numerous refugee situations in the mid-to-late 20th century. Among these were those displaced by the partition of India and Pakistan in 1947; the Cuban communist revolution refugees of 1959, many of whom migrated to southern Florida; Vietnamese refugees fleeing the war; victims of wars in Algeria, Congo, Nigeria, and Angola in Africa; Cold War refugees from Eastern Europe; and post–Cold War refugees from the Balkans who fled from genocide and other atrocities.

THE VIETNAMESE BOAT PEOPLE

The Vietnam War, which was waged between the communist government of North Vietnam and the United States–backed government of South Vietnam, lasted for more than 20 years. The fighting was bitter and deadly, and many non-combatants had their lives permanently impacted. Thousands of Vietnamese who tried to flee to safer countries were called the "Vietnamese boat people" because they tried to escape by piling into shoddy vessels. The following is the story of one such group of refugees:

> In the waning days of April 1975, Carina Hoang and her family hunkered down inside a cramped bomb shelter and listened to the rockets scorching the skies above Bien Hoa. From time to time the children dashed outside, to go to the bathroom or grab a morsel of food, and then retreated to the bunker. North Vietnamese troops had already advanced within three miles of Saigon, just half an hour's drive away, and the U.S. military had launched a frantic evacuation of the capital. "When things started to quiet down, my mom put all of us in the car and started to drive to Saigon," said Carina. "At that point, we had lost touch with our father"—a lieutenant colonel in the South Vietnamese military—"we didn't know what had happened to him and we couldn't wait for him. So we went to Saigon and stayed at my mom's friend's house and started to look for ways to leave the country."

Palestinian Refugees

Thousands of Jews fled persecution in Europe during and after World War II, and the results of this mass migration have affected politics in the Middle East right up to the present. Many fled to their ancestral homeland, a narrow strip of territory—formerly called Palestine—that sits along the southeastern Mediterranean Sea. Palestine was ruled by the British Empire, which had taken control after the fall of the Ottoman Empire. This was called the British Mandate of Palestine, but the British planned to withdraw from Palestine in 1948. Before this withdrawal was set to occur, however, they severely restricted the flow of Jews to Palestine. In 1947, the British forcibly detained the ship *Exodus*, which carried 4,500 Holocaust survivors from France. The Jewish refugees were sent back to Europe. Despite this refoulement, in time, the floodgates opened, as

The mood, Carina says, "was fearful. You just never knew what might happen next and there's all of this speculation—people cannot trust each other, people cannot say anything without being worried it will be used against you. There was no hope, there was no freedom. It felt as if somebody pulled a rug from under your feet. Everything just changed."

A few days later, on April 30, General Duong Van Minh surrendered to the Viet Cong and the Fall of Saigon was complete. For the Hoangs and hundreds of thousands of their fellow South Vietnamese, it was the beginning of a decades-long nightmare—one that prompted one of the largest mass exoduses in modern history as political refugees fled, year after year, in rickety boats across the South China Sea. Thousands perished en route to safer shores or fell prey to marauding pirates. Many more died on uninhabited islands, victims of tropical diseases, hunger and heartbreak.[1]

1. Katie Baker, "Remembering the Fall of Saigon and Vietnam's Mass 'Boat People' Exodus," Daily Beast, April 30, 2014. www.thedailybeast.com/remembering-the-fall-of-saigon-and-vietnams-mass-boat-people-exodus.

Jewish illegal immigration to Palestine overwhelmed the system.

As the date for the British withdrawal came closer, the United Nations announced a plan to help the refugee crisis. Palestine would be divided into two states: one Arab, one Jewish. The hotly contested city of Jerusalem would be under international control, so that anyone could have access to the holy sites claimed by Muslims, Christians, and Jews alike. The Jews accepted the plan, but with reservations. The Arabs rejected it. Subsequently, civil war broke out in Palestine between Jews and Arabs, both of whom laid claim to the land for generations. As the British hastened their departure in response to the chaos of a difficult situation, the Jews, led by their first prime minister—the passionate Zionist David Ben-Gurion—declared independence and announced to the world the new State of Israel.

The result of this declaration was to be expected: Egypt, Jordan, and

The Exodus, *full of Jewish Holocaust survivors, was turned away from Palestine by British authorities.*

Syria, along with forces from Iraq, all entered Palestine. The invaders stormed into the Arab areas and Israeli settlements. Despite occasional periods of truce negotiated by neutral nations, the fighting went on for nearly a year. In the end, the newly named Israelis not only defeated

their attackers but took control over much of the disputed territory.

Ordinary citizens always suffer during periods of war, and the Palestinians, caught between the Arab invaders and the Jewish defense, were victimized. More than 700,000 Palestinians became refugees without a homeland as a result of the First Arab-Israeli War. There are various versions of how this Palestinian diaspora occurred. The Israelis argue that the Palestinians left voluntarily at the urging of Arab leaders who wanted them out of their armies' way, even though the Jews asked the Palestinians to stay and show that peaceful coexistence was possible. According to this version, the Palestinians believed Arab leaders who assured them that they could return to their lands once an Arab victory was secured.

The Palestinians have a different version of events. They believe that the Jews expelled them from their land by threat, by force, and sometimes by massacre. For the Palestinians, their 1948 expulsion from their homeland is regarded as a catastrophe. Though the United Nations has a very specific definition of a refugee, all Palestinians not living in Palestine consider themselves refugees. For the Palestinians, being a refugee is a part of their core identity.

The hundreds of thousands of Palestinians who fled unintentionally caused an international crisis. In order to provide aid for the Palestinian refugees, the United Nations created a separate entity, the United Nations Relief and Works Agency for Palestinian Refugees in the Near East (UNRWA). Since 1950, the UNRWA has been providing education, health, relief, and social services to the Palestinian refugees. When first formed, the UNRWA served approximately 750,000 Palestinian refugees in Jordan, Lebanon, Syria, the Gaza Strip, and the West Bank, including East Jerusalem. Today, 5 million Palestinians qualify for aid. About 1.5 million of these refugees live in refugee camps. According to the UNRWA, "Socioeconomic conditions in the camps are generally poor, with high population density, cramped living conditions and inadequate basic infrastructure such as

Jewish and Palestinian refugees have played a huge part in the history of Israel.

roads and sewers."[56] The remaining refugees live in their host countries and in the Israeli-occupied West Bank and Gaza Strip, often near the refugee camps.

The ongoing dispute between the Palestinians and Israelis shows no sign of resolution. The Palestinians will not accept a two-state solution (first proposed by the UN in 1947), arguing that Israeli land is theirs and they should have the right to return. They also demand reparations from Israel for being expelled in 1948. Their demands are reinforced by the UN's Resolution 194, passed in 1948, which states that Palestinian "refugees wishing to return to their homes and live at peace with their neighbours should be permitted to do so at the earliest [reasonable] date, and that compensation should be paid for the property of those choosing not to return and for loss of or damage to property which, under principles of international law or equity, should be made good by the Governments or authorities responsible."[57]

Significantly, all the Arab states in the United Nations at the time, including Egypt, Syria, Lebanon, Saudi Arabia, Iraq, and Yemen, voted against UN Resolution 194, because accepting it meant that they had to acknowledge Israel as a nation in addition to the loss of most of Palestine's land to Jewish control.

Israel has rejected much of UN Resolution 194. The Israeli government knows that it faces a threat to its existence if it allows millions of Palestinians back into Israel. It argues that Israel is the only Jewish state in the world, while the Palestinian refugees could settle in any of more than 20 Arab states. The government also argues that Israel has been kind and fair to the Palestinian people who remained in the country in 1948. The Israelis also point out that during the First Arab-Israeli War in 1948, hundreds of thousands of Jews were expelled from their homes in Arab countries, from Syria to Egypt. The claims on both sides are filled with strong emotions, suggesting that the Palestine refugee crisis will not end anytime soon.

Refugees from Afghanistan During the Soviet Invasion

In December 1979, Russian forces invaded Afghanistan, creating an instability that has echoed in the entire region well into the 2010s. More than 5 million Afghans left the country because of the invasion, most for Pakistan and Iraq, and another 2 million were internally displaced. The remaining Afghans did not surrender peacefully. The Afghan freedom fighters, called mujahideen, engaged the Soviet Red Army and fought back. The mujahideen grew out of local militias, which were led by regional warlords. These warriors engaged the Soviets all across the country. As in all wars, it was the local citizens who suffered most from the fighting. Refugee camps in Pakistan overflowed with those escaping the conflict.

The United States had been engaged in a period of détente (or reduction of hostilities) with the Soviets, but Russia's attempt at expanding its sphere of influence reopened the door to conflict. With the United States increasingly providing support and armaments (but not soldiers), the mujahideen eventually pushed the Soviets out of their country.

With the end of the Soviet war, many of the refugees returned to a devastated and poverty-stricken country and attempted to rebuild their shattered lives. However, the refugees' dilemma was not over. The Soviet withdrawal left a power vacuum and led to civil war, which in turn led to the rise of a hardline Islamic group called the Taliban. Once again, refugees flowed out of Afghanistan into neighboring countries, as well as Europe and Asia. Many more Afghans were displaced internally. In all, there were four major periods of Afghan exodus: the Soviet war in the 1980s, the Afghan Civil War in the early 1990s, the years of Taliban rule from 1996 to 2001, and the American invasion that began in 2001. During these years, Afghanistan produced more refugees than any other country in the world.

One famous novel that depicts Afghan refugees is Khaled Hosseini's *The Kite Runner*. The story of a boy growing up in Afghanistan and his eventual flight from his home country after the Soviet invasion, *The Kite Runner* sold 7 million copies in the United States alone. Amir, the protagonist, flees with his father first to Peshawar, Pakistan, and ultimately to Fremont, California. While they struggle to build a new life in the United States, they are at least out of harm's way.

With the U.S. invasion of Afghanistan in 2001, the Taliban eventually lost its hold on the country, and again, millions of refugees began to return to their home country, aided by the UNHCR. This mass migration has drained the resources of the Afghan government, which has struggled to bring back such an overwhelming influx of former citizens.

More than a million refugees remained in Pakistan, however, and nearly a million more in Iran. Recently, however, Pakistan has begun to expel the Afghans. A February 2017 report by the organization Human Rights Watch stated that

> *Pakistani authorities have carried out a campaign of abuses and threats to drive out nearly 600,000 Afghans since July 2016 … The returnees include 365,000 registered refugees, making it the world's largest mass forced return of refugees in recent years. They now face spiraling armed conflict, violence, destitution, and displacement in Afghanistan.*[58]

Forced to flee their homeland, refugees from Afghanistan are often forced into impromptu camps, such as this one in Paris.

Public Radio International has reported, "Afghan refugees now live in constant fear of officials separating them from their loved ones or deporting them to their war-torn native country that many no longer consider home."[59]

The forced return has been brutal at times. According to a 26-year-old Afghan man forced out of Pakistan with his wife and two children, "In July, 11 [Pakistani] soldiers and police came to our home at 3 a.m. They entered without asking and threw all our things on the floor. They demanded to see our refugee cards and said they were expired. Then they stole all our money and told us to leave Pakistan."[60]

Controversy has arisen over the UNHCR's role in the Afghan refugees' return to their war-torn and still unstable country. The UNHCR had

CHARLIE WILSON'S WAR

When U.S. representative Charlie Wilson—who became a supporter of the Afghans against the Soviets in the 1980s—toured some refugee camps, he was disgusted by what he saw:

> Millions of proud Afghans living in mud huts without running water or the ability to feed themselves. That month twenty thousand more had poured in— young boys and girls dressed in bright tribal clothing; the women with their faces covered. They came from the mountains and valleys of a country where their ancestors had lived for centuries, a legendary warrior nation not easy to intimidate and uproot.

> All brought horror stories with them of what had caused them to flee their country. In particular they talked of helicopter gunships that hovered over their villages—hounding them even as they fled.[1]

When Wilson later met with a group of Afghan elders, he brought them a message he thought that they wanted to hear: America would provide food, shelter, and medical care to their people. Instead of being grateful, the elders claimed they wanted weaponry to knock the invaders out. "It was at this moment that Charlie Wilson realized he was in the presence of a people who didn't care about sympathy. They didn't want medicine or charity. They wanted revenge."[2]

1. George Crile, *Charlie Wilson's War: The Extraordinary Story of How the Wildest Man in Congress and a Rogue CIA Agent Changed the History of Our Times.* New York, NY: Grove Press, 2007, p. 109.
2. Crile, *Charlie Wilson's War*, p. 111.

been giving the equivalent of $200 to returning Afghans, but beginning in 2016, they doubled the amount to $400. Many observers believe that this increase was coordinated by Pakistanis to encourage the Afghans to leave their country. The increased payment would not be nearly enough to truly help Afghans who could not return to their conflict-ridden native land, nor those who had no house or property to go back to. Yet it would encourage Afghans—desperate to escape increasing Pakistani oppression—to return to a country that was struggling to deal with the influx of people.

The refugees expelled from

Pakistan who do not want to return to Afghanistan have not found a welcoming country elsewhere. Human Rights Watch asserts that forcing the Afghans back into their homeland violates the principle of refoulement, because they are still in great danger if they are returned home. Complicating the matter, European Union countries have increasingly denied asylum to Afghans, though as many as 350,000 Afghans have sought asylum there in 2015 and 2016. "One of the poorest nations on the earth now has to deal with the fallout from Pakistan's mass forced refugee returns," Gerry Simpson, senior refugee researcher at Human Rights Watch, said. "This is not the time for some of the world's richest nations to add fuel to the flames."[61]

Endless Turmoil and Terror in Central Africa

The refugee situation in the African nation of Rwanda was no less grave, when upwards of 2 million ethnic Hutus fled the country beginning in 1994. Prior to this, members of the Hutu majority had murdered approximately 800,000 Tutsis and moderate Hutus (though estimates vary) in a genocide that began with extreme Hutu nationals. These extremists incited commoners to take up arms against their neighbors. When the Tutsi Rwandese Patriotic Front (RPF), a rebel movement based in Uganda that had first attacked Rwanda in 1990, mounted an offensive and took control of the country, the genocide ended. Then, the Hutu exodus commenced. The perpetrators of the genocide fled the country along with civilian refugees. According to historian Jennie E. Burnet, "They took with them everything that could move, including trucks, cars, windows, doors, and even light switches and intentionally destroyed [Rwandan] infrastructure such as buildings bridges, and government records as they withdrew."[62] As Thomas P. Odom, a U.S. Army intelligence officer on the scene, reported, "One assumes refugees are the wretched of the earth, persecuted unjustly until they flee oppression … Not true here. Aside from the very young children—meaning under age eight—thousands of the [Hutu] refugees … were killers."[63]

The Hutu refugees were crowded into camps in what was then called Zaire but is now called the Democratic Republic of the Congo. They did not go far, and with good reason. These huge, crowded camps were close to the Rwandan border and provided a foothold from which the extremist refugees in the camp could launch attacks on Rwanda. As historian Gérard Prunier wrote, "From the beginning these camps were an uneasy compromise between genuine refugee settlements and war machines built for the reconquest of power in Rwanda"[64]

This Rwandan refugee crisis, sometimes called the Great Lakes refugee crisis, was the result of decades of fighting between the Hutus and Tutsis. The dynamics of the refugee camps and their proximity to Rwanda ensured that the fighting would not end. Though international aid organizations had largely ignored the horrific genocide, now that the situation had produced a full-blown refugee crisis, help appeared from almost everywhere. The United Nations and various non-governmental agencies stepped in to provide all the aid normally expected in a typical refugee situation. These groups could only do so much. Shortly after the refugees arrived in Zaire, a cholera epidemic broke out. Odom estimated that 100,000 Rwandans died as a result.

Many Hutu refugees took no part in the violent genocide. They simply wanted to escape the fighting.

Because of the decades of ethnic violence behind the Hutu exodus, the entire Rwandan situation was far from typical. "The refugees settled in their camps in perfect order, under the authority of their former [genocidal] leaders, ready to be used for further aims. As Joël Boutroue wrote from his experience as a senior UNHCR staff member in the camps, 'Discussion with refugee leaders … showed that exile was the continuation of war by other means.'"[65]

The UNHCR attempted to organize a Hutu refugee return to Rwanda in September 1994, and some did initially make their way back. However, the refugee camp's Hutu leaders, made up of former soldiers, henchmen, and other Hutu extremists, cut off the flow, preferring to use the masses for their own violent goals. They even threatened the aid workers. By early 1995, the attempts to move Hutus back had virtually stopped.

The Hutu refugees attempted to construct some version of a normal life in the camps. As Prunier observed, "Too normal perhaps. In the five camps around [Zaire] there were 2,324 bars, 450 restaurants, 589 shops of various kinds, 62 hairdressers, 51 pharmacies … four photographic studios, three cinemas, two hotels … There were camp information bulletins and even newspapers. And of course, there were the soldiers."[66]

In Rwanda, angered by the extremist Hutus turning their refugee camps into military organizations, leaders began to order strikes against them. The subsequent violence sent many of the refugees streaming back to Rwanda, where authorities arrested and jailed thousands of those suspected of being participants in the Tutsi genocide. Many thousands of those Hutus not arrested were simply murdered as they returned.

The Rwandan government had pledged to go beyond the ethnic divide between Hutu and Tutsi, but this was hard to accomplish. Millions of Hutus had not taken part in the 1994 genocide, but the government and Tutsi survivors tended to blame all Hutus. This was not surprising, due to the extent and horrors of the genocide, but this attitude continued to divide the country and prevent healing. Consequently, the violence did not end. Many of the Hutus who returned after the refugee camps waged guerrilla warfare against the government, continuing the instability in Rwanda.

The Rwandan genocide set in motion a sequence of events in the Great Lakes region of Africa that has resonated into the 21st century. Zaire (renamed the Democratic Republic of the Congo), site of the Hutu refugee camps, collapsed in the 1990s, as that country, too, experienced destabilization in the aftermath of the Rwandan genocide and increasing ethnic violence. From 1997 to 2003, the country was plunged into civil war. Additionally, the Congolese army battled with Rwandan forces and rebel groups near the Rwandan border.

Conflicts between multiple armed groups continue to this day as they battle with the government for control of the resource-rich eastern provinces.

CHAPTER FIVE

THE 21ST CENTURY

According to the United Nations, there are currently more refugees and displaced persons worldwide than ever before. As of June 2017, the UNHCR estimates that there are 65.6 million forcibly displaced persons in the world, of which 22.5 million fall into the UNHCR guidelines for refugee status. Another 10 million are classified as stateless people. More than 5 million of these people are Palestinian refugees. The Middle East has been in turmoil for much of recent history, and the destabilization of the region since the September 11, 2001, terrorist attacks and the subsequent U.S. wars in Afghanistan and Iraq have added greatly to the number of refugees and has had ramifications worldwide. Unrest and civil war continue in the Great Lakes region of Africa as well. The UNHCR reports that 55 percent of those classified as refugees worldwide (not including Palestine, for which the United Nations has a separate aid entity) came from three countries: 5.5 million from Syria, 2.5 million from Afghanistan, and 1.4 million from South Sudan (Darfur). The UNHCR estimates that nearly 30,000 people are forced to flee from oppression and violence every day.

New crises unfold continually. One of the most recent is the still evolving Rohingya refugee crisis in Myanmar, which has seen more than half a million ethnic minorities flee the country. The refugee crisis in Syria is also making headlines around the world.

Syria

The situation in Syria is extremely complicated. Many different groups are involved. The civil war that has been raging for years pits President Bashar al-Assad's government forces against rebel groups. In some ways,

This photograph shows a protest by Rohingya refugees.

this conflict can be described as a conventional proxy war. A proxy war is when two countries, in this case the United States and Russia, do not fight openly with one another but use another country's conflict to mask their hostility. Russia has sided with the violent al-Assad regime, and the United States has provided support to the rebels in Syria. Add in the Islamic State in Iraq and Syria (ISIS)

insurgency that has taken large areas of land in the north and east, and at times, no side is completely sure of whom they are fighting against. Both the civil war and the rise of ISIS have led to the current refugee crisis, in which millions of Syrian civilians have been either internally or externally displaced.

The tragic face of the war and the subsequent refugee crisis appeared in a picture, now famous, of a young Syrian boy, three-year-old Alan Kurdi, whose dead body washed up on the shore of a Turkish beach in 2015. The boy had fled with a group of other Syrians who were attempting to reach the Greek island of Kos. The photo prompted outrage on social media, and many liberal politicians across Europe called for a solution, or at least a more empathetic response to the Syrian crisis. Many others, however, have hardened their hearts against the refugees, claiming they take European jobs and promote terrorism. Neither of these fears is based on evidence.

As the Syrian conflicts have intensified during the past few years, the refugees, who were unable to find employment and housing in nearby countries, began to look toward Europe as a viable alternative. Many Syrian refugees desire to go to Germany,

Syrian refugees in Jordan are shown here collecting supplies from the UNHCR.

Austria, Sweden, or Norway, western European states with generous immigration policies and social benefits. To do so, they must make it through some hazardous terrain. Bulgaria was the common route from Turkey into the European Union (EU), and once there, refugees were formerly able to apply for admission into the EU. In 2014, Bulgaria, aiming to stop the influx of those from the Middle East, erected a nearly impenetrable barbed wire fence. This barrier has prevented many refugees from making it through the area, but they have still tried to reach the EU by other methods—each more dangerous than the last.

Despite the tragedy and sadness of the ongoing refugee crisis, there are examples of compassion and caring. One such example comes from the American Midwest. Sullivan High School in Chicago, Illinois, has become a melting pot of immigrants, having taken in 89 refugees in 2017 alone, many of them Syrian. Formerly a failing school, the influx of refugees has rejuvenated Sullivan. Chad Adams, the principal, is impressed by his new students: "I had never really met kids from all over the world before," he said. "You get to know these kids and you see that they have an appreciation for a free education that sometimes Americans take for granted."[67] Fitting in as a refugee in an American high school is not always easy, but the alternative is worse. One Syrian student, who had only been in the United States for a few months, said "she misses the smell of jasmine in her native Syria but not the sound of bombs."[68]

The refugee students do fit in, some very quickly. Sarah Quintenz, a teacher at Sullivan, claimed "she has watched Muslims exchange hijabs for braids. She's seen girls who never wore makeup before suddenly paint their lips bright red and boys who came in with a buttoned-up look start sagging their pants."[69]

Africa, Again

The terrible African events such as the genocide in Rwanda and the subsequent war in Zaire did not end with the 20th century. Right up to the present day, Sub-Saharan Africa has been rife with conflict and refugee crises. Perhaps the most well-known worldwide is the crisis in Darfur, a region in the west of Sudan. There, militias known as the Janjaweed, which may or may not have been government-backed, marauded through the country, indiscriminately killing people, raping women, ransacking and burning villages, pillaging supplies, and stealing or destroying livestock and crops.

In the process, hundreds of thousands of people have been displaced internally or fled Darfur, often for the nearby country of Chad. Former U.S. Secretary of State Colin Powell used the word "genocide" to describe the situation in 2004, as did his successor,

Lopez Lomong, one of the countless refugees from the violence in Sudan, eventually settled in America and made the U.S. Olympic track team.

REFUGEES IN AMERICA

In 2016, the United States admitted more refugees from the Democratic Republic of the Congo (DRC) than even those from war-torn Syria. State department figures for that year show that 16,370 refugees were admitted from the Democratic Republic of the Congo compared with 12,587 Syrian refugees.

These numbers may "reflect an easier passage for those from DRC, a majority Christian country, through the stringent vetting process refugees must undergo to enter the United States," Kathleen Newland, a senior fellow at the Washington, D.C.–based Migration Policy Institute claimed. Syrian refugees, who are overwhelmingly Muslim, have faced additional scrutiny during the presidency of Donald Trump. "We have been extremely sensitive to the possibility of people who have been involved with militia groups, with rebel groups from Syria coming in through the refugee program,"[1] Newland argued.

The Democratic Republic of the Congo refugee figure was the highest from any foreign country. After the DRC and Syria, the most refugees admitted to the United States in 2016 were from Myanmar, Iraq, and Somalia.

1. "US accepts more refugees from DRC than Syria amid warnings over militants," *Guardian*, October 3, 2016. www.theguardian.com/world/2016/oct/03/refugees-drc-congo-us-syria.

Condoleezza Rice. However, the nature of events in Darfur was not always clear: "If this is a genocide, it doesn't look very much like those we've known before," wrote one reporter, "instead, it is shadowy, informal; the killings take place offstage. It is the destruction of a people in a place where it is virtually impossible to distinguish incompetence from conspiracy."[70]

As is often the case in genocidal events, the violence in Darfur left countless orphaned children. Among these were the so-called Lost Boys of Sudan, comprising more than 20,000 youngsters who migrated in large groups to nearby countries such as Ethiopia and Kenya, where they found aid in refugee camps. However, the arrival of so many unsupervised young boys put a tremendous stress on the already bulging camps. The boys had to be housed, fed, and educated. Many of these boys spent the majority of their youth in such

In recent years, there have been huge numbers of refugees coming from the Great Lakes region of Africa, which includes the DRC.

camps. In 2001, almost 4,000 boys were brought to the United States with the help of organizations such the International Rescue Committee (IRC), an organization dedicated to helping refugees. The Lost Boys settled in many different cities across the United States.

Civil war raged in Sudan during the early 21st century, but in 2005, a peace agreement was signed that led to the creation of a separate country—South Sudan. The peace did not last, however. At the end of 2013, civil war again broke out, and many of the refugees who had returned to the country now found themselves involved in another violent conflict.

The international community that was so fixated on the Sudanese crisis has been much less involved in the Democratic Republic of the Congo's (DRC) dire refugee situation. Perhaps this is a result of a limited amount of resources, or perhaps it is just refugee fatigue. Nevertheless, one of the great humanitarian crises of the last few years has occurred in the DRC. The crisis began in 2016, as a tribal chieftain took offense that his authority was not recognized by the central government. He called for an open rebellion. The chieftain was killed shortly thereafter, but his followers pledged to avenge his death.

Since that time, more than 1.3 million people have been displaced by the violence. Unlike the civil wars in Darfur and Rwanda, there has been little assistance to those fleeing the escalating violence in the DRC. Helping refugees is expensive and requires a lot of volunteers or government organizations, which can be difficult to coordinate, especially with the number of refugees around the world today.

The UNHCR has reported that by October 2017, there were more than half a million refugees from the DRC in more than 11 African countries. In one of those strange twists that can occur when violence is widespread, there are also around 526,000 people from other African nations who are seeking asylum within the DRC. According to the UNHCR, those arriving in nearby Zambia "report extreme brutality, with civilians being killed, women raped, property looted and houses set alight"[71] back in their native land. These refugees come mainly from the DRC provinces of Haut-Katanga and Tanganyika. Thousands of refugees arrived in Zambia from the DRC in September 2017 alone. The UNHCR has reported:

Some 60 per cent of those arriving in Zambia are children. Many show signs of malnutrition. Malaria, respiratory problems, dysentery and skin infections are common among the refugees, who are in urgent need of protection and life-saving support. After they are registered by the Zambian authorities, most are relocated to the Kenani transit centre in Nchelenge district, about 90 kilometres from the border. Some of the new arrivals remain close to the border, waiting for their families to cross.[72]

The refugees are aided by the Zambian government, the UNHCR, and the Zambian Red Cross. These groups distribute hot meals and identify those with special needs. Additionally, they provide psycho-social support for survivors of abuse and violence. "The humanitarian response team is delivering basic items, including tents, plastic sheeting, mosquito nets, blankets, buckets, hygiene kits and soap. Temporary shelters are being erected, boreholes are being drilled for drinking water and temporary latrines are being constructed."[73] Even so, with more DRC refugees flooding the camps daily, a stronger international response is needed to meet their needs. Though some Congolese refugees have made it to the United States and European countries such as Sweden, Denmark, and Belgium, most remain in refugee camps on the African continent.

AN UNCERTAIN FUTURE

Refugee crises do not occur in isolation. Decisions by state leaders spark wars; civilians become collateral damage and then become refugees. They grow increasingly desperate. They often risk their lives and the lives of their children in order to escape to another, hopefully safer country. They can become targets for con men, slave traders, and other criminals.

When the Islamic extremist group al-Qaeda attacked the United States on September 11, 2001, U.S. president George W. Bush responded by invading Afghanistan and Iraq, hoping to root out al-Qaeda, the Taliban, and Iraq's dictator, Saddam Hussein. These actions, however, destabilized the region. Saddam Hussein's fall can be linked directly to the rise of the cruel and dangerous group ISIS, which filled a void left in northern Iraq and then spread into Syria. Its rise, and continued violence in Iraq, Afghanistan, and Syria, has led to the refugee crisis that has displaced tens of millions and sent many millions more seeking asylum in foreign lands, from the Middle East and Europe to the United States and Canada.

The majority of people in other countries recognize suffering and display empathy. They raise money for the refugees and welcome them into their countries. However, an incident such as an act of aggression or terrorism by a former refugee can lead to a backlash among the population. They turn on the refugees. They harden their hearts. Such is the case in Europe and the United States, as hardline right-wing groups spread a message of fear and mistrust of foreigners. These people argue that the country must be kept safe, and their message resonates with those who are afraid of sharing their country with groups of people who do

Many people living in potential host nations feel empathy toward refugees.

not share their skin color or their religious beliefs.

A Complex Problem

There have been several prominent terrorist attacks by refugees and the children of refugees in modern history. When two refugees, one from Iraq and a second from Syria, set off an improvised bomb on a London subway train in September 2017, one British newspaper columnist was quick to claim that Donald Trump was right to propose restricting the flow of refugees into America. The attack was "a godsend to every single foreigner-hating Islamaphobe [person afraid of Muslims]," wrote British journalist Sean O'Grady, "who will seize on this … and say 'I told you so.' It … offers the perfect excuse to ban [refugees] from entering this country, no matter how pitiful they appear."[74] Clearly, such attacks have the effect of making life even more difficult for asylum seekers and those organizations that help them. When the perpetrator is a refugee, as was the case in two unrelated attacks in Germany in 2016—one by a Syrian refugee and another by an Afghan refugee—fuel

Far-right nationalist marchers in Poland are shown here. Marches such as this one, which are often anti-refugee, have become a more common sight in recent years.

is added to the fire. In an uncertain world, honest, law-abiding refugees, who are themselves escaping from violence, already have enough challenges ahead of them. As O'Grady wrote, "we will not stop terror in London by kicking blameless families of Syrians out of the country."[75]

Nevertheless, many governments, including those of the United States, Germany, Denmark, Poland, the United Kingdom, and others, are developing a fear of accepting refugees. The overwhelming numbers of refugees seeking asylum in Europe and America has fueled suspicion and mistrust. Far-right, anti-immigrant groups have reared their heads across Europe and America. In 2016, Denmark instituted harsh new laws attempting to slow the flow of immigrants to a country that once was among those most accepting of refugees. Far-right French politician Marie Le Pen made waves in France by running on an anti-immigrant platform before losing to Emmanuel Macron. Germany's Alternative for Germany (AfD), Italy's Northern League, the Freedom Party (PVV) in the Netherlands, and Hungary's Jobbik all operate on platforms that oppose refugees and other immigrants. In November 2017, 60,000 Poles marched in support of white nationalism and in opposition to Islam. The march's sponsors included the National Radical Camp, an anti-Semitic group that blames wealthy Jewish people for encouraging refugees to flee to Europe. In the United States, a far smaller group of about 300 white nationalists marched in Tennessee in October 2017, specifically opposing refugee resettlement in the state.

Ongoing Issues

Clearly, the way forward for refugees worldwide is thorny, full of hazards and hatred. There are also many people who have and will continue to step forward to aid those in distress. Humans have always known how to treat foreigners in need and how to do the right thing. The Greek concept of *xenia*, the mandate to extend hospitality to the foreigner, goes back thousands of years.

However, such noble ideas have been largely forgotten by many first-world countries in the 2010s. In the first year of the Trump administration, American refugee admission quotas were cut almost in half, to fewer than 50,000. Regional caps have been set: "19,000 for Africa, 17,500 for the Near East and South Asia [including most Middle Eastern countries], 5,000 for East Asia, 2,000 for Europe and Central Asia, and 1,500 for Latin America and the Caribbean."[76] Trump has been openly critical of Obama's more liberal refugee policy, especially the acceptance of Syrian refugees, saying, "We have no idea who these people are, we are the worst when it comes

Syrian refugees often arrive in Greece by boat.

to paperwork. This could be one of the great Trojan horses."[77]

Across the ocean from the United States, refugee arrivals in Europe have decreased 57 percent in 2016 to 2017 from previous figures, and Middle Eastern refugees have grown more desperate:

More people are taking the most dangerous route through the Central Mediterranean. Along this route, smugglers are making the journey incredibly dangerous by "forgoing boats for rubber dinghies, using less fuel and preventing refugees from carrying much drinking water," human rights groups [report].[78]

Jordan, Lebanon, and Turkey have taken in millions of refugees in the 2010s, while Germany, under Angela Merkel's leadership, has accepted around 1 million since 2015. However, 86 percent of the world's refugees are taken in by developing countries, with more than a quarter of them being hosted in the world's poorest countries. According to the United Nations, "more than half of the world's out-of-school refugees are in seven countries where 'governments are already struggling to educate their own children' including Chad, Democratic Republic of the Congo, Ethiopia, Kenya, Lebanon, Pakistan, and Turkey."[79]

"The U.S. has led the world for 70 years and it's hard to think of an issue more important than refugees for the U.S. to lead now,"[80] argued Ryan Crocker, a former U.S. ambassador to numerous Middle Eastern countries. If the United States cannot increase its total of refugee admissions, he added, "we are probably moving away from American leadership on this issue."[81] Trump administration officials claim that they are focusing on protecting the United States by preventing refugees from entering, but there is growing opposition to these claims.

Given this new American philosophy, it remains to be seen where worldwide leadership on refugee issues will emerge going forward.

Notes

Introduction:
The Refugee in History

1. Quoted in Michele Kelemen, "Fact Check: Donald Trump and Syrian Refugees," NPR, June 15, 2016. www.npr.org/sections /parallels/2016/06/15/482184991/fact-check-donald-trump-and-syrian-refugees.

2. Quoted in Greg Miller, Julie Vitkovskaya, and Reuben Fischer-Baum, "'This deal will make me look terrible': Full transcripts of Trump's calls with Mexico and Australia," *Washington Post*, August 3, 2017. www.washingtonpost.com/graphics/2017/politics/australia-mexico-transcripts/?utm_term=.7061cda5088f.

3. Frederick A. Norwood, *Strangers and Exiles: The History of Religious Refugees*, vol. 1. Nashville, TN: Abingdon Press, 1969, p. 22.

4. Norwood, *Strangers and Exiles*, vol. 1, p. 22.

5. Norwood, *Strangers and Exiles*, vol. 1, p. 22.

6. USA for UNHCR, "What Is a Refugee?" accessed December 21, 2017. www.unrefugees.org/refugee-facts/what-is-a-refugee.

7. Gil Loescher, "Refugees: A Global Human Rights and Security Crisis," in *Human Rights in Global Politics*, Tim Dunne and Nicholas J. Wheeler, eds. Cambridge, UK: Cambridge University Press, 1999, p. 234.

8. Alexander Betts and Paul Collier, *Refuge: Rethinking Refugee Policy in a Changing World*. New York, NY: Oxford University Press, 2017, p. 4.

9. Gil Loescher, *Beyond Charity: International Cooperation and the Global Refugee Crisis*. New York, NY: Oxford University Press, 1993, p. 6.

10. Quoted in Gil Loescher, "Human Rights and Forced Migration," in *Human Rights: Politics and Practice*, Michael Goodheart, ed. Oxford, UK: Oxford University Press, 2016, p. 317.

11. Quoted in Gil Loescher, "Human Rights and Forced Migration," p. 317.

12. Loescher, *Beyond Charity*, p. 131.

13. Betts and Collier, *Refuge*, p. 4.

Chapter One:
Early Refugees
14. Loescher, *Beyond Charity*, p. 32.

15. Gil Loescher, Alexander Betts, and James Milner, *UNHCR: The Politics and Practice of Refugee Protection into the 21st Century*. New York, NY: Routledge, 2008, p. 1.

16. Robert Garland, *Wandering Greeks: The Ancient Greek Diaspora from the Age of Homer to the Death of Alexander the Great*. Princeton, NJ: Princeton University Press, 2014, p. 198.

17. Robert Garland, *Wandering Greeks*, p. 15.

18. Robert Garland, *Wandering Greeks*, p. xv.

19. Robert Garland, *Wandering Greeks*, p. 6.

20. Richard Miles, "What the Romans can teach us about refugees," *Guardian*, June 24, 2011. www.theguardian.com/commentisfree/2011/jun/24/roman-refugees-battle-adrianople.

21. Eric Scigliano, "What We Can Learn From the Refugee Crisis That Doomed the Roman Empire," *Observer*, October 6, 2016. observer.com/2016/10/what-we-can-learn-from-the-refugee-crisis-that-doomed-the-roman-empire.

22. Miles, "What the Romans can teach us about refugees."

23. Norwood, *Strangers and Exiles*, vol. 1, p. 114.

24. Norwood, *Strangers and Exiles*, vol. 1, p. 140.

25. Massimo Livi-Bacci, *A Short History of Migration*, Carl Ipsen, trans. Cambridge, UK: Polity Press, 2010. PDF e-book.

26. Feroz Ahmad, *Turkey: The Quest for Identity*. Oxford, UK: Oneworld, 2014. PDF e-book.

27. Suraiya Faroqhi, *The Ottoman Empire: A Short History*, Shelley Frisch, trans. Princeton, NJ: Markus Wiener Publishers, 2004. PDF e-book.

Chapter Two:
Early 20th-Century Refugee Movements
28. Edward Said, "Reflections on Exile," in *Reflections on Exile and Other Essays*. Cambridge, MA: Harvard University Press, 2003, p. 173.

29. Edward Said, "Reflections on Exile," p. 173.

30. Chase Gummer, "Migration in Europe," *Wall Street Journal* Online, accessed December 26, 2017. online.wsj.com/ww1/migration-in-Europe.

31. Quoted in Peter Gatrell, *A Whole Empire Walking: Refugees in Russia During World War I.* Bloomington, IN: Indiana University Press, 1999, p. 5.

32. Gummer, "Migration in Europe."

33. Dmitri Volkogonov, *Trotsky: The Eternal Revolutionary*, Harold Shukman, trans. New York, NY: The Free Press, 1996, p. 213.

34. Erik R. Scott, "How the Russian Revolution turned refugees into political pawns," *Washington Post*, July 6, 2017. www.washingtonpost.com/news/made-by-history/wp/2017/07/06/how-the-russian-revolution-turned-refugees-into-political-pawns/?utm_term=.47d17ab3cb5d.

35. Zinaida Zhemchuzhnaia, "The Road to Exile," in *In the Shadow of Revolution: Life Stories of Russian Women from 1917 to the Second World War*, Sheila Fitzpatrick and Yuri Slezkine, eds. Princeton, NJ: Princeton University Press, 2000, p. 103.

36. Zhemchuzhnaia, "The Road to Exile," p. 103.

37. Andrew Finkel, *Turkey: What Everyone Needs to Know.* Oxford, UK: Oxford University Press, 2012, p. 176.

38. Finkel, *Turkey*, p. 176.

39. Quoted in Reşat Kasaba, *A Moveable Empire: Ottoman Nomads, Migrants & Refugees.* Seattle and London: University of Washington Press, 2009, p. 139.

40. Fridtjof Nansen, *Armenia and the Near East.* New York, NY: Duffield & Company, 1928, pp. 308–309.

Chapter Three:
World War II and "Displaced Persons"

41. Gilbert Jaeger, "On the history of the international protection of refugees," International Review of the Red Cross, September 2001, p. 727.

42. Jaeger, "On the history of the international protection of refugees," p. 728.

43. United States Holocaust Memorial Museum, "United States Policy Toward Jewish Refugees, 1941–1952," accessed December 26, 2017. www.ushmm.org/wlc/en/article.php?ModuleId=10007094.

44. Daniel A. Gross, "The U.S. Government Turned Away Thousands of Jewish Refugees, Fearing That They Were Nazi Spies," Smithsonian.com, November 18, 2015. www.smithsonianmag.com/history/us-government-turned-away-thousands-jewish-refugees-fearing-they-were-nazi-spies-180957324.

45. Gross, "The U.S. Government Turned Away Thousands of Jewish Refugees."

46. Gross, "The U.S. Government Turned Away Thousands of Jewish Refugees."

47. Charles Simic, interview with J. M. Spalding, August 1998. *Cortland Review*, August 1998. www.cortlandreview.com/issuefour/interview4.htm.

48. Charles Simic, "Refugees," in *A People's History of World War II: The World's Most Destructive Conflict, As Told by the People Who Lived Through It*, Marc Favreau, ed. New York, NY: The New Press, 2011, pp. 260–261.

49. Simic, "Refugees," p. 263.

50. Quoted in Motoko Rich, "Charles Simic, Surrealist With Dark View, Is Named Poet Laureate," *New York Times*, August 2, 2007. www.nytimes.com/2007/08/02/books/02poet.html.

51. Ishaan Tharoor, "The forgotten story of European refugee camps in the Middle East," *Washington Post*, June 2, 2016. www.washingtonpost.com/news/worldviews/wp/2016/06/02/the-forgotten-story-of-european-refugee-camps-in-the-middle-east.

52. Quoted in Tharoor, "The forgotten story of European refugee camps in the Middle East."

53. Tharoor, "The forgotten story of European refugee camps in the Middle East."

Chapter Four:
The Late 20th Century

54. United Nations, "Basic Facts about the United Nations." New York, NY: United Nations Department of Public Information, 2004, p. 261.

55. United Nations, "Basic Facts," p. 261.

56. UNRWA, "Palestine Refugees," accessed December 28. 2017. www.unrwa.org/palestine-refugees.

57. UNRWA, "Resolution 194," accessed December 28, 2017. www.unrwa.org/content/resolution-194.

58. Human Rights Watch, "Pakistan: Mass Forced Returns of Afghan Refugees," February 17, 2017. www.hrw.org/news/2017/02/13/pakistan-mass-forced-returns-afghan-refugees.

59. Valerie Plesch and Naila Inayat, "Pakistan wants millions of Afghan refugees gone. It's a humanitarian crisis waiting to happen," Public Radio International, March 30, 2017. www.pri.org/stories/2017-03-30/pakistan-wants-millions-afghan-refugees-gone-its-humanitarian-crisis-waiting.

60. Quoted in Plesch and Inayat, "Pakistan wants millions of Afghan refugees gone."

61. Quoted in Human Rights Watch, "Pakistan: Mass Forced Returns of Afghan Refugees."

62. Jennie E. Burnet, *Genocide Lives in Us: Women, Memory, and Silence in Rwanda*. Madison, WI: University of Wisconsin Press, 2012, p. 5.

63. Thomas P. Odom, *Journey into Darkness: Genocide in Rwanda*. College Station, TX: Texas A&M University Press, 2005, p. 105.

64. Gérard Prunier, *Africa's World War: Congo, the Rwandan Genocide, and the Making of a Continental Catastrophe*. Oxford, UK: Oxford University Press, 2009, p. 25.

65. Prunier, *Africa's World War*, p. 24.

66. Prunier, *Africa's World War*, p. 26.

Chapter Five:
The 21st Century

67. Quoted in Elly Fishman, "Welcome to Refugee High," *Chicago*, June 6, 2017. www.chicagomag.com/Chicago-Magazine/June-2017/Welcome-to-Refugee-High.

68. Fishman, "Welcome to Refugee High."

69. Fishman, "Welcome to Refugee High."

70. Scott Anderson, "How Did Darfur Happen?" *New York Times*, October 17, 2004. www.nytimes.com/2004/10/17/magazine/how-did-darfur-happen.html.

71. UNHCR, "DRC violence drives more than 3,300 Congolese into Zambia in a month," October 3, 2017. www.unhcr.org/en-us/news/briefing/2017/10/59d34a2e4/drc-violence-drives-3300-congolese-zambia-month.html.

72. UNHCR, "DRC violence drives more than 3,300 Congolese into Zambia in a month."

73. UNHCR, "DRC violence drives more than 3,300 Congolese into Zambia in a month."

Epilogue:
An Uncertain Future

74. Sean O'Grady, "Focusing on whether the Parsons Green bomber was a refugee is shamelessly Islamophobic, not to mention pointless," *Independent*, September 17, 2017. www.independent.co.uk/voices/

parsons-green-bomb-tube-terrorism-islamophobia-refugees-a7951286.html.

75. O'Grady, "Focusing on whether the Parsons Green bomber was a refugee is shamelessly Islamophobic, not to mention pointless."

76. Michelle Mark, "The Trump administration will drop the refugee cap to 45,000—the lowest in decades," *Business Insider*, September 27, 2017. www.businessinsider.com/trump-considers-reducing-us-refugee-admissions-cap-to-lowest-level-in-decades-2017-9.

77. Quoted in Tal Kopan, "Donald Trump: Syrian refugees a 'Trojan horse,'" CNN, November 16, 2015. www.cnn.com/2015/11/16/politics/donald-trump-syrian-refugees/index.html.

78. Esther Yu Hsi Lee, "One year on, here's how UN member states have failed and succeeded to help refugees," ThinkProgress, September 19, 2017. thinkprogress.org/unga-refugees-one-year-15454749cb71.

79. Esther Yu Hsi Lee, "One year on, here's how UN member states have failed and succeeded to help refugees."

80. Quoted in Esther Yu Hsi Lee, "One year on, here's how UN member states have failed and succeeded to help refugees."

81. Quoted in Esther Yu Hsi Lee, "One year on, here's how UN member states have failed and succeeded to help refugees."

For More Information

Books

Bauman, Stephan, Matthew Soerens, and Issam Smeir. *Seeking Refuge: On the Shores of the Global Refugee Crisis.* Chicago, IL: Moody, 2016.
> Three experts from World Relief, a global organization serving refugees, offer a practical guide to the current global refugee crisis.

Betts, Alexander, and Paul Collier. *Refuge: Rethinking Refugee Policy in a Changing World.* New York, NY: Oxford University Press, 2017.
> This book discusses how society can move beyond seeing refugees as a burden and empower them to help themselves and fit in.

Evans, Kate. *Threads: From the Refugee Crisis.* London, UK: Verso, 2017.
> This graphic novel vividly combines fiction and accurate reporting to depict a refugee camp in northern France.

Frank, Matthew J., and Jessica Reinisch. *Refugees in Europe, 1919–1959: A Forty Years' Crisis?* London, UK: Bloomsbury, 2017.
> This is a history of 20th-century Europe as seen through the lens of its many refugee crises.

Haines, David W. *Safe Haven? A History of Refugees in America.* Sterling, VA: Kumarian Press, 2010.
> This book draws on a wide range of historical material to provide a portrait of this crucial component of American immigration and how America has interacted with the rest of the world.

Hollenbach, David. *Driven from Home: Protecting the Rights of Forced Migrants.* Washington, DC: Georgetown University Press, 2010.
> This book discusses how best to protect and assist the growing number of persons forcibly displaced from their homes from a human rights perspective.

Kingsley, Patrick. *The New Odyssey: The Story of the Twenty-First-Century Refugee Crisis.* New York, NY: Norton, 2017.
> This resource contains stories of refugees who undergo arduous journeys in order to arrive at new countries and the trials they endure along the way.

Miliband, David. *Rescue: Refugees and the Political Crisis of Our Time*. New York, NY: TEDbooks, 2017.

This is a passionate plea to the world to take action concerning the current refugee crisis by the head of the International Rescue Committee.

UNICEF. *Uprooted: The Growing Crisis for Refugee and Migrant Children*. New York, NY: UNICEF, 2016.

This report presents global data about forcibly displaced children, including where they are born, where they move, and some of the dangers they face along the way. It highlights the challenges faced by child refugees.

World Bank. *Forcibly Displaced: Toward a Development Approach Supporting Refugees, the Internally Displaced, and Their Hosts*. Washington, DC.: World Bank Publications, 2017.

The international financial institution looks at the current refugee crisis from a socioeconomic perspective to encourage new thinking about helping those in need.

Websites

Cultural Orientation Resource Center (COR)

www.culturalorientation.net

This organization, which tries to meet the needs of American refugee newcomers, has a large amount of publications and videos about refugees.

The European Council on Refugees and Exiles (ECRE)

www.ecre.org

ECRE is a European network of 99 non-governmental organizations in 40 European countries that protects and advances the rights of refugees, asylum seekers, and displaced persons.

International Rescue Committee (IRC)

www.rescue.org

This organization provides support to those whose lives are shattered by conflict and disaster. Its website includes numerous reports on refugee crises.

The United Nations High Commissioner for Refugees (UNHCR)

www.unhcr.org/en-us

The world's most important refugee aid organization has a website full of up-to-date information on the current refugee crisis and what is being done to alleviate it worldwide.

United Nations International Children's Emergency Fund (UNICEF)
www.unicef.org
    This United Nations organization serves the world's children, and its website contains materials focusing on young people, including the effect on children of recent crises, such as that of the Rohingya people.

The U.S. Committee for Refugees and Immigrants
refugees.org
    This organization produces the annual *World Refugee Survey*, which presents information on refugees, internally displaced persons, and asylum seekers.

The U.S. Department of State Bureau of Population, Refugees, and Migration
www.state.gov/j/prm
    This U.S. government organization within the State Department works with the international community to develop humane and long-term solutions to displacement.

Index

Picture Credits

Cover Anadolu Agency/Contributor/Anadolu Agency/Getty Images; pp. 6–7 (background) Zacharie Rabehi/EyeEm/EyeEm/Getty Images; p. 6 (left) UniversalImagesGroup/Contributor/Universal Images Group/Getty Images; pp. 6 (right), 47, 51 Everett Historical/Shutterstock.com; p. 7 (left) Pictures from History/Bridgeman Images; p. 7 (center left) SilvaAna/Shutterstock.com; p. 7 (center right) serkan senturk/Shutterstock.com; p. 7 (right) Sk Hasan Ali/ Shutterstock.com; p. 10 De Visu/Shutterstock.com; p. 11 BULENT KILIC/ Contributor/AFP/Getty Images; p. 14 Juanmonino/E+/Getty Images; p. 17 ZU_09/DigitalVision Vectors/Getty Images; p. 19 PHB.cz/ Shutterstock.com; p. 22 DEA/G. DAGLI ORTI/Contributor/De Agostini/ Getty Images; pp. 24–25, 38–39 Hulton Archive/Stringer/Hulton Archive/ Getty Images; p. 27 Tinseltown/Shutterstock.com; p. 28 Peter Hermes Furian/ Shutterstock.com; pp. 30–31 Buyenlarge/Contributor/Archive Photos/Getty Images; pp. 33, 86 NurPhoto/Contributor/NurPhoto/Getty Images; p. 34 Ulf Andersen/Contributor/Hulton Archive/Getty Images; p. 36 Central Press/ Stringer/Hulton Archive/Getty Images; p. 40 Grethe Ulgjell/Alamy Stock Photo; p. 44 Bettmann/Contributor/Bettmann/Getty Images; p. 49 Arthur Lookyanov/Shutterstock.com; p. 53 WENN Ltd/Alamy Stock Photo; p. 56 Margaret Bourke-White/Contributor/The LIFE Picture Collection/Getty Images; p. 59 Juriaan Wossink/Shutterstock.com; pp. 64–65 GPO/Handout/ Hulton Archive/Getty Images; p. 66 Chris Ware/Stringer/Hulton Archive/ Getty Images; p. 69 JOEL SAGET/Staff/AFP/Getty Images; p. 72 Langevin Jacques/Contributor/Sygma/Getty Images; p. 76 The India Today Group/ Contributor/The India Today Group/Getty Images; p. 77 Jeff J Mitchell/Staff/ Getty Images News/Getty Images; p. 79 Kevin Morris/Contributor/Corbis Sport/Getty Images; p. 81 Giles Clarke/Contributor/Getty Images News/Getty Images; p. 85 DANIEL LEAL-OLIVAS/Stringer/AFP/Getty Images; pp. 88–89 Nicolas Economou/Shutterstock.com.

About the Author

Gary Wiener is a retired educator, having spent 33 years as an English teacher, department head, assistant principal, and district curriculum leader. He holds a Ph.D. from the University of Rochester and lives in nearby Pittsford, NY. His 28 Greenhaven and Lucent books include *Understanding the Adventures of Huckleberry Finn*, *Readings on J.K. Rowling*, *Lacrosse: Science on the Field*, and *The United States and Russia: A Cold and Complex History*. He is the father of two children, Michael and Mollie, and is married to the fabric artist Iris Schifren Wiener.